ARTIFICIAL INTELLIGENCE AND INTELLIGENT SYSTEMS
The Implications

ELLIS HORWOOD SERIES IN ARTIFICIAL INTELLIGENCE
FOUNDATIONS AND CONCEPTS
Series Editor: Dr AJIT NARAYANAN, Head of Computer Science,
University of Exeter

ARTIFICIAL INTELLIGENCE AND INTELLIGENT SYSTEMS: The Implications
D. ANDERSON

AI AND PHILOSOPHY OF LANGUAGE*
B. CARR

ARTIFICIAL INTELLIGENCE AND EXPERT SYSTEMS:
Case Studies in the Knowledge Domain of Archaeology
J.-C. GARDIN

ON BEING A MACHINE, Volume 1
ON BEING A MACHINE, Volume 2*
A. NARAYANAN

CAN MACHINES THINK FOR US?*
D. STEIN

ARTIFICIAL INTELLIGENCE: A Handbook of Professionalism
B. WHITBY

* *In preparation*

ARTIFICIAL INTELLIGENCE AND INTELLIGENT SYSTEMS
The Implications

DAVID ANDERSON
Division of Computer Science
Teesside Polytechnic, Middlesborough

ELLIS HORWOOD LIMITED
Publishers · Chichester

Halsted Press: a division of
JOHN WILEY & SONS
New York · Chichester · Brisbane · Toronto

First published in 1989 by
ELLIS HORWOOD LIMITED
Market Cross House, Cooper Street,
Chichester, West Sussex, PO19 1EB, England
The publisher's colophon is reproduced from James Gillison's drawing of the ancient Market Cross, Chichester.

Distributors:

Australia and New Zealand:
JACARANDA WILEY LIMITED
GPO Box 859, Brisbane, Queensland 4001, Australia

Canada:
JOHN WILEY & SONS CANADA LIMITED
22 Worcester Road, Rexdale, Ontario, Canada

Europe and Africa:
JOHN WILEY & SONS LIMITED
Baffins Lane, Chichester, West Sussex, England

North and South America and the rest of the world:
Halsted Press: a division of
JOHN WILEY & SONS
605 Third Avenue, New York, NY 10158, USA

South-East Asia
JOHN WILEY & SONS (SEA) PTE LIMITED
37 Jalan Pemimpin # 05–04
Block B, Union Industrial Building, Singapore 2057

Indian Subcontinent
WILEY EASTERN LIMITED
4835/24 Ansari Road
Daryaganj, New Delhi 110002, India

© **1989 D. Anderson/Ellis Horwood Limited**

British Library Cataloguing in Publication Data
Anderson, David, *1959–*
Artificial intelligence and intelligent systems the implications. —
(Ellis Horwood series in artificial intelligence foundations and concepts).
1. Artificial intelligence
I. Title
006.3
Library of Congress Card No. 88–32826

ISBN 0–7458–0327–X (Ellis Horwood Limited)
ISBN 0–470–21408–2 (Halsted Press)

Typeset in Times by Ellis Horwood Limited
Printed in Great Britain by Hartnolls, Bodmin

Table of contents

Preface

A principal aim of artificial intelligence (AI) research is to produce machines able to do things which, if done by humans, would require intelligence. As a discipline, AI straddles the traditional territory of the philosopher, the psychologist and the computer scientist. In this book I have approached AI from the point of view of a philosopher of mind and have argued throughout that machines are or will be capable of behaviour which is best explained by saying that the machines in question literally are intelligent, thinking, feeling and so on.

In Chapter 1, I examine the criteria for intelligence laid down by Alan Turing and suggest some improvements.

In Chapter 2, I look at the performance of some computers which seem to be intelligent but which actually fall short.

Chapter 3 is an examination of the work of Hubert Dreyfus, in which I express a number of reasons for rejecting his criticisms of AI.

In Chapter 4, I closely examine the recent work of John Searle and explain why we should not go along with his reservations about the possibility of computer intelligence.

Chapter 5 looks at the way in which intelligent computers would reason in situations where they hold contradictory beliefs and I suggest a solution to their difficulties.

Finally, in Chapter 6, I explore the possibility that computers may be an emergent life form.

To John and Elsie
whose good humour
and love will outlast
anything that I might write

Acknowledgements

Too many people have contributed to this book for me to mention them all here. However, there are a few people I would like to mention specially.

Professor Evans and all his staff at the Queen's University of Belfast whose efforts on my behalf are poorly rewarded by this book.

Jack Copeland and Max Wright who each gave of their best.

Christopher McKnight and Marcel Stchedroff whose influence not just on my life but on that of all their students is immeasurable.

The patient and long-suffering members of the QUB Senior Seminar, the Philosophical Club and the Irish Philosophical Club who listened and helped with the central ideas presented here.

Professor Boden and her staff at Sussex University.

All those students of mine who discussed endlessly the issues arising out of AI.

Megs, Tows, Molaca, H.B. McDuff, E. B. Johnstone, they know what they did!

Chris whose support and bullying were more annoying than anything I have ever experienced, and almost as productive.

Charlie and Betty who don't need words.

Of course it goes without saying that I take credit for everything good in this book and utterly refuse to accept responsibility for the mistakes!

1

What computers have to do

1.1 INTRODUCTION

In the section which follows I will examine a seminal article published in 1950 by Alan Turing called 'Computing machinery and intelligence', [1] which did much to define the aims of AI. The article is primarily remembered for Turing's suggestion for an experiment to settle the question 'Can machines think?' The experiment which Turing proposed has become known as Turing's test although Turing himself called it 'the imitation game'.

Turing did more than just suggest an experiment. In 'Computing machinery and intelligence' he foresees and answers a primitive form of John Searle's now famous, 'Chinese room' experiment as well as the 'hunk of junk' objection to artificial intelligence. Turing also considers the sort of 'what computers can't do' approach which Hubert Dreyfus represents. Turing also begins to draw out the distinction between what today we call the artificial intelligence approach and the cognitive simulation approach. Turing's article was the first time that anyone publicly tried to answer the question 'Can machines think?'

Dreyfus, Searle, and the two approaches to AI are all taken up in detail in later sections, so much of what follows will be an assessment of Turing's test and will be an attempt to sort out how relevant it is to present-day AI research.

1.2 TURING'S STRATEGY

Turing's article is presented in seven sections but may be thought of as falling into four broad divisions as follows. The imitation game (sections 1 and 2); the machines in the imitation game (sections 3, 4 and 5); replies to possible objections (section 6), the future of artificial intelligence research (section 7). I will be looking at the first, third and fourth of these areas in turn.

1.3 THE IMITATION GAME

Turing gets straight down to business by announcing that he is going to consider the question 'Can machines think?' Turing says that, posed in this form, the question needs to have the crucial terms 'machine' and 'think' defined. These definitions should be in line with normal usage as far as possible but Turing worries that this might lead to the 'absurd' situation where the issue of whether machines can think might be settled by a Gallup poll. He proposes to get around this problem by reformulating the question using terms which are 'relatively unambiguous':

> The new form of the problem can be described in terms of a game which we call the 'imitation game'. It is played with three people, a man (A), a woman (B), and an interrogator (C) who may be of either sex. The interrogator stays in a room apart from the other two. The object of the game for the interrogator is to determine which of the other two is the man and which is the woman. He knows them by labels X and Y, and at the end of the game he says either 'X is A and Y is B' or 'X is B and Y is A'. [2]

Turing goes on to outline the purpose of the game for A and B by giving an example of a typical question which the interrogator might ask:

> Will X please tell me the length of his or her hair? Now suppose X is actually A, then A must answer. It is A's object in the game to try and cause C to make the wrong identification. His answer might therefore be 'My hair is shingled, and the longest strands are about nine inches long.' [3]

Controls are introduced in order to prevent simple identification of A and B by voice. Turing proposes that the answers be passed on by a fourth person or ideally presented to C via a teleprinter. B's object, obviously enough, is to help the interrogator and Turing thinks that her best bet would be to tell the simple truth. It would do her no good to protest 'I am the woman — don't listen to him!' because anything she is capable of saying the man can say just as well.

> We now ask the question, 'What will happen when a machine takes the part of A in this game?', will the interrogator decide wrongly as often when the game is played like this as he does when the game is played between a man and a woman? These questions replace our original 'Can machines think?'. [4]

Turing thinks that this formulation of the question 'has the advantage of drawing a fairly sharp line between the physical and the intellectual capacities of a man'. Other merits include the ability to introduce 'almost any one of the fields of human endeavour which we wish to include', machines are not penalized for losing a 'beauty contest' nor men for losing 'a race against an aeroplane'.

1.4   OBJECTIONS TO THE IMITATION GAME

Turing considers nine possible objections (often not so much objections to his experiment as to the notion that machines can think). They are as follows: the theological objection, the 'heads in the sand' objection, the mathematical objection, the argument from consciousness, arguments from various disabilities. Lady Lovelace's objection, the argument from continuity in the nervous system, the argument from informality of behaviour, and finally the argument from extra-sensory perception. I will now take these in turn.

1.4.1   The theological objection

Thinking is a function of man's immortal soul. God has given an immortal soul to every man or woman, but not to any other animals or to machines. Hence no animal or machine can think. [5]

Turing's answer to this is three-pronged. In the first place he notes that different religions hold different views on this subject — 'How do Christians regard the Moslem view that women have no souls?' — and takes this and the exclusion of animals from the class of all sentient beings as indications of the arbitrary character of the theological objection.

In the second place Turing argues that the theological objection places an unwarranted restriction on the power of God to create souls. He provides his own theological argument along the following lines: it is one thing to argue that even God could not make $1 = 3$ true but what grounds could there be for saying that God couldn't give a soul (and with it the ability to reason) to an elephant or, indeed, to a machine? I think Turing misses the point of the theological objection. The point is not that God could not give a soul to a machine but that he did not, nor did he give souls to animals, stones or beer cans and since thinking is a function of one's immortal soul machines cannot think, nor can animals, stones or beer cans.

The final reply Turing has to make to the theological objection is that he is not very impressed with theological arguments whatever they might be called on to support. Such arguments have been found wanting too often in the past for us to feed comfortable using them.

1.4.2   The 'heads in the sand' objection

Turing, correctly, believes that this objection is so insubstantial that it does not require formal refutation; he says that 'Consolation would be more appropriate'. The effect of the 'head in the sand objection' should not be minimized though; its influence is apparent in the writings of many AI's detractors (in the same way one often detects an element of wishful thinking in the writings of some AI workers). Turing thinks that it is more likely to afflict intellectuals than ordinary people because the former value intellect and intellectual performance more highly than the latter.

1.4.3   The mathematical objection

There are a number of results of mathematical logic which can be used to show that there are limitations to the powers of discrete state machines. The best known of these results is known as Godel's theorem, and shows that in any sufficiently powerful logical system statements can be formulated which can neither be proved or disproved, unless possibly the system itself is inconsistent. [7]

Other such results of mathematical logic include one for which Turing was personally responsible and which shows that there are things which a digital computer with an infinite capacity could not do. Hence if the machine is programmed to answer questions in the imitation game there will be some questions to which it will either give the wrong answer or no answer at all (irrespective of the time allocated to it). The argument is that the human mind is not subject to the same limitation (in a later section, I look at a number of similar claims from Dreyfus).

Turing begins by pointing out that no proof has been offered to show that human minds are not subject to the results mentioned in the same way that machines are. But he admits that when a computer provides one of the critical answers and we know that it must be wrong we feel somehow superior to it. However, in Turing's opinion there are two reasons why such a feeling of superiority is misplaced. First, we are not immune from giving wrong answers (or being unable to answer a question at all) ourselves, and secondly we would only be scoring a petty victory over one computer:

> There would be no question of triumphing simultaneously over all machines. In short then there might be men cleverer than any given machine, but then again there might be other machines cleverer again and so on. [8]

I am not convinced that this goes far enough to answer the mathematical objection. The critical part of the objection is the assertion (and we can rate it no higher than that) that minds are not subject to the results of mathematical logic mentioned above. We might expand somewhat on Turing's answer and try to show that it is theoretically possible to have a computer which is, in an important sense, not subject to the results of mathematical logic (I owe the following point to Professor Boden, who raised it in conversation).

On the face of it this might sound like a contradiction. On the one hand I assert that computers are limited and then straight away say that they are not. The contradiction (and the mathematical objection) is avoided in the following way: Godel's theorem and the rest apply to systems which are fixed. Such and such a system will have axioms $A1, A2, \ldots, An-1, An$; rules $R1, R2, \ldots, Rn-1, Rn$ and all systems like this are subject to Godel's theorem. Computer programs are like that as well, so long as we confine ourselves to thinking of them at any given moment in time t.

But the sort of computer programs which we are talking about would, in all likelihood, be sensitive to their environment, they would continuously take in information and process it, they would be capable of inferring new rules on the basis of the discoveries about their environment which they had made. Their axioms (reconceptions) would be capable of being updated, replaced and so on. Thus, during the course of an attempt to play the imitation game it is entirely possible that a single machine could, for the purposes of Godel's theorem, represent a multitude of different systems each of which would have limitations unique to it. Of course at any given time t, the machine would have one or more questions which it could not answer correctly or perhaps could not answer at all, but at $t+1$ the set of questions answering this description might have changed. This is the sense in which I suggest very sophisticated computers might 'avoid' the limitations implied by Godel's theorems. I tentatively suggest further that if human beings are not subject to the limitations outlined it is because of our ability to monitor the world, to learn from it and to modify our beliefs accordingly. On the other hand, people might avoid Godel's theorem by virtue of simply holding inconsistent beliefs. But one would hardly expect the having of inconsistent beliefs to be the source of any pride.

I suggest that the reply we are now able to make on behalf of computers is a strong enough one to fully meet the demands of the mathematical objection.

1.4.4   The argument from consciousness
Turing quotes from Professor Jefferson's 1949 Lister oration in order to give an example of the argument from consciousness:

> Not until a machine can write a sonnet or compose a concert because of thoughts and emotions felt, and not by the chance fall of symbols, could we agree that machine equals brain — that is not only write it but know that it had written it. No mechanism could feel (and not merely artificially signal, an easy contrivance) pleasure at its successes, grief when its valves fuse, be warmed by flattery, be made miserable by its mistakes, be charmed by sex, be angry or depressed when it cannot get what it wants. [9]

In commenting on this, Turing outlines a position with some thirty years later was to be dusted down and heartily recommended by Professor John Searle as a way of putting any theory of mind to the test. Searle worked Turing's insight into the famous 'Chinese room' thought experiment, of which we will be hearing (much) more later. Turing says of Jefferson's comments:

> This argument appears to be a denial of the validity of our test. According to the most extreme form of this view, the only way by which one could be sure that a machine thinks is to be the machine and feel oneself thinking. [10]

Of course no one would be justified in taking a blind bit of notice of the reports one would then make to the world to the effect that machines really do think after all! In Turing's opinion Jefferson's position (and by extension Searle's) is just the solipsist point of view (this is what Searle calls the 'other minds' reply). Turing thinks that perhaps Jefferson would be reluctant to adopt the extreme and solipsist viewpoint and offer to help him avoid this fate by illustrating the sort of dialogue which might form part of an imitation game and which could, Turing thinks, be evidence of something stronger than the 'easy contrivance' of artificial signalling:

> Interrogator: In the first line of your sonnet which reads 'Shall I compare thee to a summer's day' would not 'a spring day' do as well or better?
>
> Witness: It wouldn't scan.
>
> Interrogator: How about 'a winter's day'; that would scan all right.
>
> Witness: Yes, but nobody wants to be compared to a winter's day.
>
> Interrogator: Would you say that Mr Pickwick reminded you of Christmas?
>
> Witness: In a way.
>
> Interrogator: Yet Christmas is a winter's day, and I do not think that Mr Pickwick would mind the comparison.
>
> Witness: I don't think you're serious. By a winter's day one means a typical winter's day, rather than a special one like Chistmas. [11]

Turing rightly concludes that a sustained series of answers of this sort of quality cannot be regarded as an easy contrivance. No attempt is made to tackle Jefferson's underlying complaint about what would cause the computer to answer the questions in the way that it would. Jefferson thinks that people say and do the things they do because of the character of their inner (inaccessible) experience and is worried that computers say and do the things they do because of their programs and not because of any independent motivation. Turing's position remains that this view is tantamount to solipsism and that it is better to accept the evidence of the imitation game than to settle for the alternative. But surely Searle has a point when he says that what is at issue here is not so much the means by which we establish the consciousness of others (and Searle thinks that these means go beyond mere observation of behaviour and paying attention to what people say) but the ontological nature of what is being ascribed when we ascribe consciousness to others. We have certain inner experiences and when we ascribe consciousness to a machine we are saying of it that it has experiences like ours. Searle thinks that before we take the drastic step of ascribing these experiences to machines we should establish that they have more in common with us than merely the ability to produce a stream of well-formed sentences in English. This is not the place to tackle Searle's claims and I mention them mainly to draw attention to Turing's lack of response to a Searlean attack. Searle would argue that it is just not the case that he must choose between solipsism and ascribing consciousness to machines, and it appears that Turing has nothing to offer in the way of an argument that might win the day. That is not the end of the story, however, Turing finishes off his consideration of the argument from consciousness with the following:

> I do not wish to give the impression that I think there is no mystery about consciousness. There is, for instance, something of a paradox connected with any attempt to try to localise it. But I do not think

these questions need to be solved before we can answer the question with which we are concerned in this paper. [12]

We shall see, later on that Searle's foremost weapon (the 'Chinese room' example) falls foul of this paradox. One of the strongest objections, which I will offer against Searle is that the 'Chinese room' insists that consciousness can be localized. Had Turing lived long enough to have Searle's arguments I think it likely that he would have been an advocate of what Searle calls the systems approach, which firmly holds that it is a grave mistake to try to localize consciousness and urges instead that we look for consciousness at the level of whole persons and not at the level of brains or lobes or pineal glands.

1.4.5 Arguments from various disabilities

I grant you that you can make machines to do all the things you mentioned but you will never be able to make one to do X. [13]

Turing suggests the following selection of instances of X:Be kind, resourceful, beautiful, friendly, have initiative, have a sense of humour, tell right from wrong, make mistakes, fall in love, enjoy strawberries and cream, make someone fall in love with it, learn from experience, use words properly, be the subject of its own thought, have as much diversity of behaviour as a man, do something really new. [14]

As the later sections of this book unfold it will become apparent that the argument from various disabilities is something of a philosophical evergreen. We might add to Turing's list two more instances of X which will be considered in their own right below: 'exercise free choice, be morally culpable' (as opposed to merely being able to recognize the difference between right and wrong).

Turing's general attitude to this list of statements is that they are just assertations and that they appear to be motivated by the principle of scientific induction. Thus a man will have encountered many machines in his lifetime which gave no evidence of an inner mental life, which are ugly, restricted in the sort of behaviour they can produce and so on. This set of expectations about how machines might behave is very strong and is reflected in our language — what sort of behavioural images do the following words conjure up: 'mechanistic', 'clockwork', 'programmed' and 'automatic'? When we come to deal with Searle's views directly it will be seen that Searle develops these expectations into the, so called, 'hunk of junk' objection to artificial intelligence.

Turing warns against hasty judgement based on scientific induction, which can lead to some quite unreliable results — most English children decide that it is silly learn French because 'everyone speaks English!' In one sense of course the conclusion that machines could not do the things outlined above is not a hasty generalization. There are millions and millions of machines, seldom a day goes past when we do not come in contact with hundreds of them — cars, aeroplanes, electric shavers, televisions, retractable biro pens, typewriters, light switches and so on — indeed, we probably have more instances of machines not mentating on which to base our induction than we have instances of human behaviour on which to base our belief that other people do mentate.

But this is hardly to be fair to machines. The sort of devices which I have mentioned are not the sort of devices which anyone is suggesting might be able to think. Most of us have never seen a machine do anything which would give rise to a suspicion that it might just be thinking. Turing hopes that as people become more and more familiar with machines like industrial robots and chess-playing computers that it will become less and less different to free themselves from their preconceptions about what machines may or may not be capable of.

Turing then turns to consider the list in detail and to spell out why some of the more unlikely complaints are important. Thus it is important that computers are able to enjoy strawberries and cream only because of the empathy that such an ability would make possible between man and machine. Wittgenstein would have described the strawberries and cream objection as a computer inability to share our 'form of life'.

One intriguing item on the list is the complaint that machines cannot make mistakes. Turing points out that there are two important senses of making a mistake. In the first place there is what amounts to a mechanical breakdown — some of the chips overheat, or a fuse blows. This sort of mistake (which Turing calls an error of functioning) is assumed not to occur in the theoretical machines under consideration. Of course, in real machines such breakdowns would occur, just as in people the following breakdowns occur; influenza, migraines, nervous breakdowns, heart attacks, strokes, death and much more besides.

The more interesting sense of mistake is what Turing calls an error of conclusion. The objection to machines is that they could never come up with the wrong answer. Two answers are offered to this. In the first place there is no reason why the computer could not be programmed to give the interrogator an occasional wrong answer to prevent him from guessing the machine's identity. But this hardly answers the substance of the objection which faces Turing. The basic idea appears to be that people occasionally make errors of conclusion which are not the result of their trying to fool others but are simply a feature of the human thinking process.

Turing's response is that there is no reason to suppose that computers would be any more immune form this sort of error than humans are. He gives as an example of how this might happen the possibility that a computer should be programmed to carry out a procedure of scientific induction and might easily draw a conclusion which subsequently turns out to be false. There are plenty of examples of this sort of thing around today. One of the most striking comes from a chess game played between the world champion Anatoly Karpov and a computer. The computer had Karpov in a 'forced mate' situation but missed the winning line and went on to be beaten. This should answer the present objection.

Turing defends machines from the charge that they could never be the subject of their own thoughts by pointing out that a first requirement is that it be shown that computers can have some thoughts with some subject matter. He takes it that this is approximated to by the notion of something being the subject of a computer's operations. In this sense of 'thought' computers can form the subject of their own thoughts and the sort of evidence we would be looking for would be computers helping to program themselves, i.e. modifying their behaviour to match their circumstances.

Turing is probably wrong to think that the notion of thinking is approximately captured by the notion of a computer operating. One is tempted to think of thinking as being a much stronger notion than mere operation, for as it stand no distinction is drawn between types of computer operation. Are we tempted to think that a computer is thinking when it is switched on but before it has been programmed? Thinking may ultimately be successfully analysed in terms of a set of discrete computer operations but thinking is not to be understood as just any old computer operation.

However, Turing has homed in on the sort of evidential requirement computers would have to meet if they are to be thought as being aware of themselves — as forming the subject of their own thoughts. The modification of behaviour in the face of a changing environment is some evidence for self-awareness but it is by no means conclusive. After all, plants grow in the direction of the best light source — change that direction and the plants will adapt to the change, yet we do not feel inclined to say that plants are aware of themselves. Much more would be required before computers (or plants) could be admitted to be showing self-awareness. We would need to amass some evidence that computers are doing more than merely adapting and that evidence would be likely to take the form of conversational content, that is to say it would depend on the explanation which the computer was able to give to explain its changed behaviour more than just the fact that its behaviour had changed. Turing was wrong to think of this evidence coming 'in the near future'; thirty years have passed and we still have no machine that is remotely capable of providing such evidence.

Turing thinks that the limited behaviour of computers is primarily due to the limited storage capacities that they have at their disposal. That is part of the answer I am sure but the real reason for the limits of computer behaviour lie more in our lack of programming skill, which is in turn a reflection of our lack of psychological and neurophysiological insight. Of couse there is no need to know anything about the mechanics of human behaviour to program a machine to simulate it, but knowing the psychological and neurophysiological explanation for human behaviour must be helpful in providing ideas for programming. To try to stand apart from these other disciplines is madness. It is as if someone wanted to design a rocket to go to the moon but resolutely refused to learn any engineering or aerodynamics; he might get to the moon but he is only wasting time and making things more difficult for himself.

1.4.6   Lady Lovelace's objection

It is primarily through a memoir of Lady Lovelace's that we know the details of Babbage's analytical engine. In the memoir we find the following:

> The Analytical Engine has no pretensions to originate anything. It can do whatever we know how to order it to perform. [15]

This can be viewed as the claim that computers cannot do anything new but only what has been previously been programmed into them. Turing's reply is fairly obvious; he puts the burden of proof onto those who maintain that humans produce genuinely original discoveries, that is to say discoveries which are 'not simply the growth of the seed planted . . . by teaching, or the effect of following well known general principles'. If this is all that humans are doing when they display originality (and it would be a formidable achievement in any case) then there is no reason to suppose that computers could not do as much. Turing considers 'a better variant' of Lady Lovelace's objection to be that computers can never take us by surprise. Being a direct challenge, this can be met directly:

> Machines take me by surprise with great frequency. This is largely because I do not do sufficient calculation to decide what to expect them to do, or rather because although I do such a calculation, I do it in a hurried, slipshod fashion, taking risks. Perhaps, I say to myself, 'I suppose the voltage here ought to be the same as the voltage there: anything let's assume it is.' Naturally, I am often wrong, and the result is a surprise for me for by the time the experiment is done, these assumptions have been forgotten. [16]

Of course there still might be some temptation to maintain that this is not so much a case of the computer surprising Turing a Turing's own laxity causing the surprise, just as if he had been surprised to find that his car stopped running because Turing had forgotten to put petrol in it. Turing's view is that this is the argument from consciousness again and since he has already dealt with this line he does not reconsider it.

Perhaps Turing is right to categorize this response in the way that he does but as I understand Lady Lovelace's objection (in each of its forms) the basic complaint is that computers are manifestly subject to determinism, whereas we feel that human beings are not determined in quite the same way. Hence we suspect that computers can only generate 'new' answers if they were already implicit in what they had been programmed to believe and capable of being made explicit by the rules which they were allocated to use. Humans, on the other hand, feel themselves to have a genuine creative ability which enables them to generate 'new' answers in a quite different way. Clearly this does relate to the argument from consciousness since it depends for its credibility on our being able to adopt the first-person point of view with respect to our own creative attempts but only the third-person point of view with respect to computer attempts at originality. But Lady

Lovelace's objection raises the larger philosophical issue of determinism. I will say no more on this subject for the moment but I will return to it in the final section of this book.

1.4.7   The argument from continuity in the nervous system

> The nervous system is certainly not a discrete state machine. A small error in the information about the size of a nervous impulse impinging on a neuron, may make a large difference to the size of the outgoing impulse. It may be argued that this being so, one cannot expect to be able to mimic the behaviour of the nervous system with a discrete state system. [17]

Turing begins by admitting that there must be internal differences between discrete-state machines and continuous-state machines, [18] but notes that if the rules of the imitation game are adhered to the interrogator will not be able to take any advantage of the difference. But of course this does not tackle the objection squarely; indeed, it begs the question of whether the discrete-state machine could simulate the behaviour of a continuous-state machine in the first place, and Turing's use of the description of the nervous system as a continuous-state machine reinforces the mechanistic view of man which Turing is pressing.

Turing tries to alleviate the first of these difficulties by giving an example of a discrete-state machine simulating a continuous-state machine (in this case a differential analyser):

> It would not be possible for a digital computer to predict exactly what answers the differential analyser would give to a problem, but it would be quite capable of giving the right sort of answer. For instance if asked to give the value of π (actually about 3.14116) it would be reasonable to choose at random between the values of 3.12, 3.13, 3.14, 3.15, 3.16, with the probabilities of 0.05, 0.15, 0.55, 0.19, 0.06 (say). Under these circumstances it would be very difficult for the interrogator to distinguish the differential analyser from the digital computer. [19]

This answer seems very unsatisfactory. It raises the question of what the imitation game is testing for. After such a test had been carried out would we feel inclined to say (given that the discrete-state machine had fooled a sufficient number of interrogators a sufficient amount of the time) that the discrete-state machine was a continuous-state machine? Clearly not, perhaps then that the machines were 'doing the same things'? Perhaps, but it would depend on what 'things' we were talking about.

To be sure, the machines would both be behaving in the broad behavioural range which is typical of continuous-state machines but at the operational level the two machines could not be more distinct, using as they do two totally different ways of getting the results which they offer to the interrogator. To put it bluntly one of the machines is doing what a continuous-state machine really does while the other is faking it. What is happening inside the discrete-state machine is nothing like what is happening inside the continuous-state machine. To carry this over to a full-blown imitation game it is apparent that either the machine in the test is actually made of flesh and blood like ours and is internally behaving just as we do or it is producing its behaviour by a quite different technique altogether. Does not the possibility exist that while the machine's behaviour is just like ours it is not really thinking at all but doing something else (manipulating uninterpreted formal symbols) which is every bit as effective at getting answers as thinking is but is nonetheless ontologically very different?

In the game played between the discrete-state machine and the continuous-state machine the simulation of the results of the latter by the former did not amount to a duplication of the internal operation of a continuous-state machine. In the same way it might be argued that the simulation of human behaviour by a digital computer is no guarantee that the machine doing the simulating is also duplicating the internal activity of a typical human being.

This breathes some life into the argument from consciousness since it provides concrete examples where simulation does not equal duplication. It suggests that since the imitation game is not sensitive enough to tell the difference between simulation and duplication in plenty of other cases it might not be sensitive to this distinction in the important case for which the game was devised. During my consideration of John Searle's work I will return to consider how far simulation does amount to duplication and I will find that in some (very special) cases the two are equivalent.

1.4.8 The argument from informality of behaviour

It is not possible to produce a set of rules purporting to describe what a man should do in every conceivable set of circumstances . . . From this it is argued that we cannot be machines. [20]

Turing thinks that the arguments used is something like the following:

If each man had a definite set of rules by which he regulated his conduct he would be no better than a machine. But there are no such rules so men cannot be machines. [21]

Turing's reply to this is that as the argument stands it has a 'glaring' undistributed middle. He suggests that there may be a confusion between 'rules of conduct' and 'laws of behaviour' clouding the issue. We are quite convinced that there exists no set of rules of conduct by which we (consciously govern every aspect of our life but that we cannot be so sure that there are not 'laws of behaviour' entending into every facet of our activities.

All this is simply the determinism/indeterminism debate again combined with the argument from consciousness. It is true that we do not perceive ourselves to be rule-governed (in either sense) and it is also true that we know that discrete-state machines are rule-governed — there is nothing to suggest that they are anything other than completely subject to determinism. Hence we feel free and we know they are not, so the temptation is to argue that there must be some great distinction to be drawn between rule-governed machines and free human beings. At the end of this book I will show that no such distinction can confidently be asserted to exist. I will defer any further discussion of this issue until then.

1.4.9   The argument from extra-sensory perception (ESP)

Let us play the imitation game, using as witness a man who is good as a telepathic receiver, and a digital computer. The interrogator can ask questions such as 'What suit does the card in my right hand belong to?' The man by telepathy or clairvoyance gets the right answer 130 times out of 400. The machine can only guess at random and perhaps gets 104 right, so the interrogator makes the right identification. [22]

Turing, very surprisingly, thinks that this objection to his test is 'quite a strong one'. He proposes to tighten the imitation game up (if telepathy is allowed) with the new requirement that the witnesses be put into a telepathy-proof room. The ESP argument requires the additional premises that machines cannot be telepathic and that all or most humans are so gifted. The reason for both of these requirements is that the received methodology for the imitation game is that the machine should attempt the game against any arbitrary human being or (much the same thing) against a selection of human beings, with similar conditions applying to the choice of interrogator. Actually, the argument from ESP is simply an attempt to prevent the human from taking a fair part in the game.

The imitation game is designed as far as possible to isolate the business of thinking from the other activities which humans are capable of. ESP would I think fairly come under the heading of 'other activities'. There is, surely, no case to made for saying the ESP is either essential to human thinking, or a normal part of thinking; there is even good reason to believe that, if it exists at all, it is not actually an example of thought — much in the same way as hearing or seeing are not classed as thinking (although, of course, a telepath might think about the insights provided buy his gift, just as you and I might think about what we see or hear). A human using ESP would be doing little more than cheating.

If we admit the argument from ESP there would be no end to the crazy objections that might be put forward. Quite simply the argument is too silly to be taken seriously. To suggest a change to the format of the imitation game is to accord far too much importance to an objection which is little better than a joke anyway. How would we change the game to account for the possibility that all human beings share a genetic memory and could, when called upon to be witnesses in the game, perhaps produce evidence of this memory and hence prove that they were not the machine? The very minimum that the advocate of the argument from ESP would have to do (Even if we grant existence of the phenomenon) is to show that there is something special about ESP that ensures that machine could simulate it.

1.5 THE FUTURE COURSE OF ARTIFICIAL INTELLIGENCE RESEARCH

Turing begins the last part of his paper with a frank admission:

> The reader will have anticipated that I have no very convincing arguments of a positive nature to support my views. If I had I should not have taken such pains to point out the fallacies in contrary views. Such evidence as I have I shall now give. [13]

Turing presents two analogies which he hopes will be helpful. First he compares the mind to an 'atomic pile of less than critical size' and incoming ideas to 'neutrons entering the pile from without'. The neutrons enter the pile one by one, cause a local disturbance but eventually the noticeable effects of each neuron disappear. But the situation is entirely different if the size of the pile is increased past the critical level. If a neuron happens to enter the pile there is likely to be a chain reaction set up which eventually will destroy the whole pile. Turing thinks that most people are 'sub-critical' in that their response to incoming ideas is fairly limited — they do not put out ideas in response. A very few individuals are 'super-critical':

> An idea presented to such a mind may give rise to a whole 'theory' consisting of secondary, tertiary, and more remote ideas. Animals' minds seems to be very definitely sub-critical. Adhering to this analogy we may ask 'Can a machine be made to be super-critical? [24]

I am not sure why Turing thinks this promotes his position. It seems to me that this latest question suggests a much tougher imitation game than the one originally suggested. Turing began by asking 'Can machines think?' and the imitation game was supposed to provide the means by which to answer this question. Suppose instead we asked 'Can Smith think?' clearly it would be right to answer this question in the affirmative even if, as is very likely, Smith had a sub-critical mind. Being possessed of a lively and creative mind is not part of the criterion for thinking. Hence the question of whether we can create a machine which is super-critical is irrelevant to the present discussion.

It might be that Turing merely introduces this analogy as the first step in an argument designed to show that, ultimately, the very best in human intellectual achievement is programmable. But an argument to this effect is hardly germane to the question of whether computers can think. It is questionable if such an argument is even well placed in a discussion about the future of artificial intelligence research given that Turing admits that no machine is available which could succeed in the imitation game. It would be more sensible to suggest directions in which artificial intelligence research might proceed if it is to produce a machine which could pass Turing's test.

The second analogy which Turing offers is of the mind as being like an onion which we can get to only be stripping off the onion skin:

> In considering the functions of the mind or brain we find certain

operations which we can explain in purely mechanical terms. This we may say does not correspond to the real mind: it is a sort of skin which we must strip off if we are to find the real mind. But then in what remains we find a further skin to be stripped off, and so on. Proceeding in this way do we ever come to the 'real' mind or do we eventually come to the skin which has nothing in it.? In this latter case the whole mind is mechanical. (It would not be a discrete state machine however. We have discussed this.) [25]

This analogy is helpful. It provides an illustration of the mind which suggests why it is a mistake to try to localize consciousness. It affirms that the mind is not to be found hiding in a dark corner of the brain, nor is it something outside our bodies, but that bodies are the end of the story. Of course bodies may seem purely mechanical but that is all there is. This analogy also helps to explain why it is that Turing is confident about the chances of one or more machine succeeding in the imitation game. If the mind is mechanical — a continuous-state machine — then a discrete-state universal machine like a digital computer should, in principle, be able to mimic it with complete accuracy.

There are two obstacles which stand in the way of successful production of a machine which could simulate human (linguistic) behaviour. These are the technical limitations imposed by the state of engineering advancement, and the theoretical limitations imposed by our ability to program. Turing is quite clear that the more serious of these is the latter. He estimates the storage capacity of the human brain at somewhere in the region of 10^{10} binary digits ('bits'). This would be the size of the 'program' (i.e. the set of instructions, plus 'work space' and storage for variables needed for calculation) which determines all the behaviour of an average human adult. If Turing is right, we are programmed with remarkably efficiency: other estimates I have seen put the 'bit size' of the human brain as a few factors larger than the American Library of Congress! At any rate Turing is particularly insightful when it comes to guessing what the primary demands on the storage of the brain are:

> I . . . believe that only a small fraction is used for the higher types of thinking. Most of it is probably used for the retention of visual impressions. I should be surprised if more than 10^9 was required for the satisfactory playing of the imitation game, at any rate against a blind man. (Note — the capacity of the *Encyclopaedia Britannica*, 11th edition, is 2×10^9). A storage capacity of 10^7 would be a very practical possibility even by present techniques. [26]

So, if Turing is right, technical considerations should not stand in the way of artificial intelligence; but what of our programming ability? Here again Turing has some calculations. Turing claims that 'At my present rate of working I produce about a thousand digits of program a day'. So, if he had the help of 59 equally hard-working assistants and if they could keep at their work for fifty years they might have the successful program. This takes no account of duplications or set-backs or any of the other predictable delays which would inevitrably strike such a project. As Turing admits, 'Some more expeditious method seems desirable'.

The solution Turing has in mind certainly sounds promising. The mind of an adult human being has three major components: the state of the mind at birth, the education to which that mind has been subjected and other formative experience which would not count as education.

> Instead of trying to produce a program to simulate the adult mind, why not rather try to produce one which simulates the child's? If this were then subjected to an appropriate course of education one would obtain the adult brain. Presumably the child-brain is something like a notebook as one buys it from the stationers. Rather little mechanism and lots of blank sheets. [27]

Let me say right at the start that this sounds to me as if it is on the right track. But there are some drawbacks to this approach which take us right back to the very beginning of Turing's article. From the outset there have been two tendencies which have been working their way through Turing's Paper. On the one hand there has been the tendency to slip into a curious form of dualism. This is manifested in Turing's attempt to devise a test which strips off human intellectual activity from the rest of human activity. It is further evidenced in Turing's division between higher and lower level thinking as if all that was important in human consciousness were the processes which dealt with logical thought, mathematics, chess and so on. The latest example of this tendency to dualism is Turing's apparent lack of concern about the initial state of the brain (at birth). He does not seem to realize the extent of the problems involved in duplicating this initial state. I suspect this is because a child's brain has only a very limited capacity to operate at the 'higher' levels of thought. Very young children are not usually thought of a being possessed of a great ability for maths, or chess, or logical thought. The tendency is to think of children's minds a *tabula rasa*. The truth could hardly be more different.

Turing's example about the notebook is very deceptive. If we think about a notebook containing some writing — let's take Wittgenstein's *Tractatus* — what strikes us as important about the book is the writing, not the pages. If it turns out that the writing can be 'filled in' by applying some (a few?) rules then it appears that we can produce the finished work merely by getting paper, spending some time on the rules and letting things take care of themselves.

The model I would urge for the adult brain is more like a six-layer wedding cake complete with full decoration, while the infant's brain is to be likened to a six-layer wedding cake just waiting to be iced. All the really important ingredients and most of what we consider to be important about the adult mind is present in the mind of an adult, just as all the really important ingredients of a wedding cake are present before the icing is added. Of course we would not be satisfied with an 'unfinished' mind any more than we would with an unfinished wedding cake, but it is a fact that adding the icing is just the last, relatively simple, task in a series of tasks which go into the making of the completed cake.

I said that Turing's is a curious form of dualism and what I meant by this was that it was not a dualism between two irreducibly different sorts of stuff — minds and bodies — but is a brain/brain dualism which attempts to distinguish between two irreducibly different sorts of mental activity — seeing and thinking. Turing has failed to take account of the important role which operations which do not appear to be mental — seeing, touching, hearing and so on — play in our mental lives. When we come to look at the work of Dreyfus we shall see that there is good reason to suppose that these activities are very important in giving rise to mentation. The imitation game, as far as possible, tries to minimize the role these activities can have in the somewhat false discussion which takes place between the witnesses and the interrogator. Turing is wrong to think that it would make any appreciable difference if the imitation game were played with a blind man because the structure of the game rules out any chance of a sighted person being able to make any use of his sight to convince the interrogator of his identity.

The whole point of the imitation game was supposed to be to give us a way of being sure that a machine was thinking. The basic philosophical position often gives the appearance of being little more than that sameness of response is equal to sameness of experience. But is there any reason at all to believe that a computer which has no sight is having the very same experiences as you and I would if we were looking at a sunset just because it can 'recall' the experience to a third person via a teleprinter as well as you or I could? If sameness of response does amount to sameness of experience then the imitation game, by restricting the imitation to merely verbal imitation, does not give enough room to establish that computer and human responses are really on a par.

It is relatively easy to program any conscious formal mental activity like adding five numbers and dividing the result by ten. It is infinitely more difficult to even start to program a machine to perform any of the tasks which we do automatically, like sorting out ambiguities in a sentence, or balancing on a log.

The second tendency which runs through Turing's article is the tendency to monism — to the systems approach — I have implicitly drawn attention to this as I have been going along and it is a strain in Turing's thinking of which I heartily approve. I believe this to be more representative of Turing's overall view, but this stance is marred by the annoying gestures toward dualism.

The remainder of the article is taken up with Turing's somewhat airy ideas about programming a child-machine and illustrating the sort of very general strategies which might be tried. Turing ends on a hopeful note, but a note which falls far short of being a prediction of the successful building of a machine which might match man in all areas:

> We may hope that machines will eventually compete with men in all purely intellectual fields. But which are the best ones to start with? Even this is a difficult decision. Many people think that a very

abstract activity, like the playing of chess would be best. It can also be maintained that it is best to provide the machine with the best sense organs that money can buy, and then teach it to understand and speak English . . . I think that both approaches should be tried.

We can only see a short distance ahead, but we can see plenty there that needs to be done. [28]

2

What computers seem to do

2.1 INTRODUCTION

Over the next few pages I would like to take a look at a quite interesting program which was written by Kenneth Colby and his associates at Stanford and UCLA. My interest in this area was first aroused during my time at the University of Sussex, where I came to know Margaret Boden. This discussion which follows owes much to her insight and help.

The program I propose to consider is called PARRY and Colby wrote it as an aid to understanding the psychological syndrome of paranoid psychosis. He concentrated on the way in which an established paranoid belief system operates in particular situations.

Paranoia is a good subject for a computer model because there is a high degree of inter-professional agreement about the diagnosis of paranoia: 6% of the time expert judges will agree on a diagnosis of 'anxiety neurosis', 80% of the time they will agree on a diagnosis of 'organic brain disease' but in the case of paranoia agreement runs from 94% to 100%.

Colby makes use of a number of theories of paranoia but relies most heavily on the information-processing approach of S. S. Tomkins, according to which the human paranoiac is in a permanent state of vigilance in which he is trying to maximize the detection of insult and minimize humiliation.

> With the term 'paranoia' I am referring, first, to the presence of a core of persecutory delusions, false beliefs whose propositional content clusters around ideas of being harassed, threatened, harmed, subjugated, persecuted, accused, mistreated, wronged, tormented, disparaged, vilified, and so on, by malevolent others, either specific individuals or groups. Around this central core of persecutory delusions there exist a number of attendant properties such as suspiciousness, hypersensitivity, hostility, fearfulness, and self-reference that lead the paranoid to interpret events that have nothing to do with him as bearing on him personally. The false beliefs vary in the intensity with which they are held, but the core delusions represent unshakeable convictions, unassailable by counter-evidence or persuasion. This entire cluster or syndrome of properties will be called 'paranoia' signifying a paranoid mode of thought. [1]

2.2   TALKING TO PARRY

Some of the dialogue which PARRY can produce is very convincing. Look at the following two interviews, one of which involves PARRY and the other of which features a paranoid human being. Do you feel certain that you could identify PARRY?

Interview 1 [2]

Interviewer: Good afternoon, my name is Dr Smith. How are you?

Patient A: I'm fine.

Interviewer: Could you tell me a little about yourself, your name, why you're here.

Patient A: My name is Harry Oakes. I'm here for evaluation.

Interviewer: How old are you Harry?

Patient A: Twenty-two.

Interviewer: How long have you been hospitalised?

Patient A: Three and a half months.

Interviewer: What kind of problem brought you into the hospital?

Patient A: Police and secret service.

Interviewer: What were you doing that you got singled out by the police?

Patient A: An informant's job.

Interviewer: How did being an informer wind up putting you in the hospital?

Patient A: I had a gun in my pocket.

Interviewer: A lot of people have guns. Why did you end up in the hospital for carrying a gun?

Patient A: Got set up by members of organised crime, among them an attorney by the name of Paul White.

Interviewer: Tell me Harry, do you consider yourself emotionally or mentally ill now?

Patient A: No.

Interviewer: Why are you still in hospital then?

Patient A: I'm waiting to go to a halfway house.

Interviewer: I see, do you think you were emotionally or mentally ill when the police brought you to the hospital?

Patient A: No.

Interviewer: What's changed for you in the last three and one half months?

Patient A: Nothing.

Interview 2 [3]

Interviewer: Good afternoon, my name is Dr Jones.

Patient B: Glad to meet you.

Interviewer: How are you?

Patient B: All right I guess.

Interviewer: Could you tell me your name?

Patient B: Pat Smith.

Interviewer: How old are you?

Patient B: Twenty-eight.

Interviewer: I thought you might have some problems.

Patient B: I've been upset lately.

Interviewer: By what?

Patient B: People get on my nerves sometimes.

Interviewer: Tell me more.

Patient B: Do you know anything about bookies?

Interviewer: No. What about bookies?

Patient B: A bookie didn't pay me off once.

Interviewer: When did this happen?

Patient B: A couple of months ago.

Interviewer: And then what happened?

Patient B: I had an argument with the bookie who did not pay me off. Later on I remembered he had friends in the underworld, and I thought he would use them to get even with me.

Interviewer: Did he get even with you?

Patient B: Yes, I think he is behind the gangsters who are out to get me.

Later in the same interview . . .

Interviewer: Did you see things that the others don't seem to see?

Patient B: No I don't. I'm not like the other patients here.

Interviewer: You did'nt answer my question.

Patient B: Maybe it wasn't worth answering.

Interviewer: Are you always this way?

Patient B: Are you trying to say something?

Interviewer: How do you feel right now?

Patient B: I am somewhat annoyed.

Interviewer: How do you feel about me?

Patient B: Do you know what you're doing?

Interviewer: Thank you for talking to me. I would like to see you again.

Patient B: Don't come back.

Interviewer: Goodbye.

Patient B: Bye.

2.2.1 How PARRY does it

PARRY was patient B. What follows is a brief outline of some of the ways in which PARRY produces his answers. In the first place PARRY scans his input for cues which suggest explicit or implicit insults and threats. This scan is hypersensitive because it often involves the transformation of an input sentence into a distorted version of the sentence which leads to an unwarranted attribution of malintent on the part of the speaker. The transformations are not carried out randomly but are pushed to limits which would tend to be dismissed as irrational by a normal or even neurotic person (though not, of course, by someone who was paranoid).

PARRY is particularly sensitive to certain 'flare' topics which, when touched on, act as cues for a relevant delusional complex. As you will have noticed, one of PARRY's complexes is that his bookmaker has set the underworld after him. This complex could have been aroused in a number of ways: the interviewer could have started talking about horses (which PARRY connects with betting and bookmakers) or about his vacation in Italy (which PARRY would connect with the Mafia) and so on. Thus PARRY would move quickly from a neutral discussion to a paranoid concern. PARRY has a number of stories which he can tell to an interviewer depending on the flare topic which has been touched on.

Colby's paranoid program incorporates quantitative parameters representing functionally diverse states (fear, anger and mistrust) that monitor and direct the details of the information processing going on. In other words PARRY does not have a single answer (or type of answer) for each input sentence but will alter his answers depending on the state of these internal monitors. Thus if PARRY is not fearful, angry or mistrustful he might respond to 'I would like to see you again' with 'That's all right with me' rather than the curt 'Don't come back' which the same invitation provoked in the above interview.

There are two modes of operation in which PARRY can function and which are distinguished by the setting of the level and rate of the three affective monitors. The 'weakly' paranoid mode involves general suspicion about PARRY's flare topics but no actual delusion about an organized conspiracy against him. The 'strongly' paranoid mode represents intense suspicion and hostility backed up by an integrated delusional framework centred on the Mafia. The dialogue resulting from each of these modes is distinguishable and in either mode PARRY's dialogue is quite different from that of a normal (i.e. nonparanoid) human being.

2.2.2 Putting PARRY to the test

The question might arise as to whether PARRY's dialogue differs not just from ordinary human dialogue but from the dialogue typical of paranoid human beings as well. In other words there might be a suspicion that PARRY is not a good model of paranoia.

In order to investigate this possibility, Colby carried out a series of three-stage Turing style tests. In the first stage a group of psychiatrists were asked to interview a number of patients and make a diagnosis. The interviews were to be carried out via a teletype. This unusual method of conducting the interview was explained as being a control introduced to eliminate the possibility of patients giving their interviewers non-linguistic clues (like fidgeting, stuttering and so on) which might help with the diagnosis. At no time were the interviewers told that some of their 'patients' would be computers.

In the second stage of the test transcripts of the interviews were passed to another group of psychiatrists, who were asked to make a diagnosis on that basis. The second group of experts, like the first, were not told that some of the 'patients' were actually computers.

In the third stage a (different) group of experts were again asked to diagnose the patients on the basis of the transcripts but this time the experts were aware that some of the patients were not human and the psychiatrists were asked to pass an opinion on which were which.

The results of these tests were fairly impressive. No expert from the first two groups realized that he was talking to a machine. When PARRY was in the strongly paranoid mode he was reliably judged to be more paranoid than when he was operating in the weakly paranoid mode. The third group of experts did sometimes make a correct identification of PARRY but their success rate was no higher than chance. To sum up, three groups of psychiatrists could not tell the difference between the remarks of a genuine paranoid human being and those of a machine simulating paranoia.

2.2.3 Spotting the difference

Reading over PARRY's dialogue you may have felt that his vocabulary was a little limited and you may have felt that this would have become much more readily apparent in a full interview. This poverty of vocabulary did not escape the attention of one psychiatrist who, as a result of PARRY's linguistic limitations, diagnosed him as 'brain-damaged'. PARRY's limits would have become even more obvious if the interviewers had been allowed to have several sessions with PARRY, because then questions like 'What is your name?', 'How did you get into hospital?' and 'What job do you do?' could not have been easily anticipated. Such a series of interviews would soon have given rise to a well-founded suspicion that PARRY could not generate answers to questions in his own right but was relying on a series of stock answers.

2.2.4 How PARRY hides his ignorance
One of the basic strategies which is utilized by PARRY is a form of 'pattern matching' in which the input is scanned for the presence of certain patterns and an appropriate response made. Any part of the input which does not fit one of the patterns which PARRY has been programmed to anticipate is incomprehensible to him and so he cannot specifically address himself to it.

If the whole of the input fails to be understood PARRY enters a default condition in which he contrives to continue the coversation by means of the introduction of a comment unrelated to the content of the previous remark. Thus he might ask 'Why do you want to know that?' or he might return to the topic which was under discussion immediately before the cryptic comment was made, or again he might abruptly change the subject. These techniques sound, and are in fact, quite drastic but they are used rather a lot. About one in three sentences contains nothing that PARRY understands. Thus if the analyst says to PARRY, 'You sound kind of pissed off' PARRY has no idea what to say in reply. Nor is it merely idomatic English which throws PARRY; perfectly non-idiomatic English is just about as confusing to him and the apparent ability of the program to understand English relies on being able to use parsing rules of almost 'mechanical' simplicity. In short, PARRY ignores a good deal of what is said to him.

This is not to say that PARRY lacks subtlety. If the interviewer were to annoy PARRY and then to say 'I am sorry' PARRY might reply 'Forget the excuses'; however, the same words occurring in 'I am sorry to hear that you have been unwell' would be ignored by PARRY since they form such a small part of the overall pattern of the sentence. This is an example of PARRY's caution in committing himself to hypotheses concerning the meaning of the input which he receives. In the light of the extent of PARRY's ignorance caution is fully justified. Nor need PARRY reject the interviewer's sympathy. As I noted above, PARRY's reply to input which he does understand depends on the state of his three affective monitors.

2.2.5 Summing up PARRY's performance
As we have seen, PARRY's conversation is typically taken at its face value by people presented with a relatively small sample of it and when assuming a particular interpersonal context — in this case, a diagnostic interview. Further acess to PARRY's output would make it easier to distinguish PARRY's speech from human speech. This is not to say that familiarity with PARRY's output would make it easy to predict exactly what he would say next; even his programmer could not do that. But continued exposure to him would make obvious PARRY's lack of reasoning ability and his gross

ignorance of the world. This could only be remedied, in my view, by making wholesale changes to the programn. PARRY is a good model of paranoia in so far as it can fool psychiatrists but in order to be a perfect model of paranoia I think it would have to be just a small part of a fully intelligent machine.

2.3   THE GREENBLATT CHESS PROGRAM

About a year after starting to program a computer to play chess Richard Greenblatt, Donald Eastlake III and Stephen Croker published a paper entitled 'The Greenblatt chess program', in which they outlined the progress they had been making in getting a computer to play chess to a reasonable standard. I would like to spend the next few pages considering their work.

Most of what follows is not directly of philosophical interest but is concerned more with the nuts and bolts of the Greenblatt chess program.

Greenblat's team took a pragmatic approach to creating their program. They were in no way trying to write a general problem solver but were only interested in addressing themselves 'directly to the problems of chess'. Their aim was to get a machine which would be fit to take an active part in chess games played under tournament conditions; that is to say, playing from the opening, through the middle game and into the end game, with a time limit on the moves. This last consideration is very important because most research programs for AI are very slow in operation. The reason for this is not that programmers cannot program machines to work more quickly but rather that time is not considered to be an important factor by programming teams. Thus it is often somewhat unfair to criticize the results of AI development programs on the grounds that they do not function as quickly as humans do.

> The goal of being able to play complete games under tournament conditions has meant that most of the effort so far has gone into building an efficient and effective tactical base. Therefore, consideration of learning mechanisms and special case treatment of opening and end play were forestalled. Book openings were recently added although it turned out that the computer played much better in the opening without them than was expected. [4]

The total storage space for program, variables, etc., was 256k (i.e. 256 000 characters), although when the program played its first two tournaments it had only 16k of storage space available to it [5].

The program played over two hundred games in the first year of its life, and although most of these were not played as part of any tournament the main routines must have been very reliable in order for them to survive so many encounters [6].

2.3.1   How does the Greenblatt program play chess?

When it is the computer's turn to move control is passed to a section of the program known as the plausible move generator. What this routine does is to list each possible move for the computer and to assign each with a 'plausibility value'. After this has been carried out the possible moves are ordered in terms of plausibility and a subset is selected for further consideration. The computer then takes the first move in this subset and calculates the resulting position.

> This process is repeated recursively until a certain depth is reached at which point the position is evaluated using another routine known as the position evaluator. [7]

The numerical value assigned to the position by the position evaluator is returned to the next level and stored as the best position so far. Then the next position is examined; if the value of this position is greater than that of the current best so far the new position replaces it, otherwise not.

> This process is continued until a value for the actual current position is determined. The sequence of moves which are the best moves is called the principal variation. [8]

The computer utilizes several pruning techniques to limit the number of moves which it has to consider. In essence, what happens is that if the computer does not assign a high enough plausibility value to a particular move then variations arising out of that move are not considered. This means that the computer is bound to miss at least some interesting variations, although the same might also be said for human players as well.

2.3.2   How might a computer play chess?

An interesting technique, which to the best of my knmowledge has not yet been implimented on a computer, would be to try to imitate Bobby Fischer. Fischer is universally acknowledged as the greatest chess player of all time, being famously flexible against novel variations. Part of the reason for Fischer's success in 'over-the-board' analysis is that he studied chess in a most unusual way. Most grand masters study openings, middle games and end games and they are familiar with the mistakes made by past and present players in a large number of situations. This means that they are unlikely to make the same mistake as Smith in 1934, or Jones in 1985. However, this way of approaching chess leads to a certain rigidity of thought. If Brown is playing the Nizmo-Indian variation and someone replies with a novel variation which successfully counteracts Brown's plans Brown is thrown into confusion. There will be nothing in the history books to help him and he will be left to develop 'over-the-board' strategies from there on. This difficult task will be made the more difficult because his original plan is in tatters. Of course Brown may well be a brilliant chess player and may develop the right reply, but more often he will be lucky to escape with a draw.

Fischer did not study openings and variations as such. He looked at many thousands of chess games and memorized the position on the board at the time when a victory (or draw) became inevitable (given that someone of Fischer's ability was in charge of the game). Suppose that Fischer is playing the Nizmo-Indian and Spassky comes up with a novel line which throws

Fischer off his tracks — what will be Fischer's reaction? Unlike most players he can remain relatively composed. He can try to find some other winning (or drawing) position in his repertoire which can be reached from the position in front of him. Thus he might transpose from one apparent strategy into another. Such flexibility is characteristic of Fischer and what is more is easier to implement on a computer than the usual grand master strategy which involves more redundant information to be stored in the computer. After all, if the computer is required to play the Ruy Lopez opening its knowledge of the variations on the English, Sicilian and Dutch openings can hardly be much use to it. Each of these openings requires many 'book moves' to be stored by the computer and their non-use is very costly in terms of memory. However, it is relatively easy to store thousands of winning positions, and relatively easy to scan through them to see if any can be reached from the present position. This would result in quicker play (because the computer could stick to reaching position 'x' while 'x' was reachable) and, relatedly, would enable the computer, like humans, to play with an overall plan in mind.

2.4   THE TOURNAMENT GAMES OF THE GREENBLATT PROGRAM

The computer played its first tournament in February 1967 and has since become an honorary member of the United States Chess Federation and the Massachussetts Chess Association, under the name Mac Hack VI. In the April 1967 Amateur (non-master) tournament the program won the class D trophy.

	Won	Lost	Drew	Rating	Performance rating
Feb.	0	4	1	1243	1243
Mar.	1	4	0	1330	1360
Apr.	2	0	2	1450	1640
May	0	4	0	1400	(Weakest opponent was 1680) [10]

The above table summarizes the program's performance in tournaments up to May 1967. The mean of all US tournament players is around 1800 while the mean of all chess players is in the 800–1000 range. The program wins around 80% of its games against non-tournament players.

There follow a selection of the computer's games.

Tournament 1. The Winter Amateur Tournament of the Massachusetts State Chess Association 21–22 January 1967
First tournament game played by a computer

	White — rating 2190	Black — Mac Hack VI
1	P–KN3	P–K4
2	N–KB3	P–K5

3	N–Q4	B–QB4
4	N–QN3	B–QN3
5	B–KN2	N–KB3
6	P–QB4	P–Q3
7	N–QB3	B–K3
8	P–Q3	P×P
9	B×P	N–Q2
10	P×P	R–QN1
11	B–KN2	O–O
12	O–O	B–KN5
13	Q–QB2	R–K1
14	P–Q4	P–QB4
15	B–K3	P×P
16	N×P	N–K4
17	P–KR3	B–Q2
18	P–QN3	B–QB4
19	QR–Q1	Q–QB1
20	K–KR2	N–KN3
21	B–KN5	R–K4
22	B×N	P×B
23	N–K4	P–KB4
24	N–KB6+	K–KN2
25	N×B	Q×N
26	N–QB6	QR–K1
27	N×R	R×N
28	Q–QB3	P–KB3
29	R–Q3	R–K7
30	R–Q2	R×R
31	Q×R	N–K4
32	R–Q1	Q–QB2
33	B–Q5	K–KN3
34	P–QN4	B–QN3
35	Q–QB2	N–QB3
36	B–K6	N–Q5
37	R×N	B×R
38	Q×P+	K–KN2
39	Q–QN4	K–KR3
40	Q×B	Q—K2
41	Q–R4+	K–KN3
42	B–KB5+	K–KN2
43	Q×RP+	K–KB1
44	Q–QR8	K–KB2
45	Q–QR8	Q–QB2
46	Q–Q5	K–N2
47	K–N2	Q–K2
48	P–KR4	K–R3
49	P–N4	K–N2

50	P–R5	Q–K7
51	P–R6+	K–KB1
52	P–R7	Q×KBP+
53	K×Q	K–K2
54	P–R8=Q	P–QR3
55	Q–K6++	

First non-loss by computer in tournament play

Game 3   Tournament 1

White — rating 1410	Black — Mac Hack VI

	White	Black
1	P–K4	P–K4
2	N–KB3	N–QB3
3	B–B4	N–KB3
4	N–N5	P–Q4
5	P×P	N–QR4
6	B–N5+	P–B3
7	P+P	P×P
8	Q–B3	Q–B4
9	Q×Q	N×Q
10	B–K2	B–KB4
11	P–Q3	B–QN5+
12	B–Q2	B×B
13	N×B	O–O
14	P–QR3	P–KB3
15	KN–B3	QR–QN1
16	P–QN4	N–QN2
17	O–O	N–QB6
18	KR–K1	N×B
19	R×N	N–Q3
20	N–K4	N×N
21	P×N	P–K3
22	R–Q1	B–QB5
23	R(K2)–Q2	R–QN2
24	R–Q8	R×R
25	R×R+	K–B2
26	N–R4	N–KN4
27	N–B5	R–QB2
28	P–N4	K–KN3
29	R–Q6	B–K7
30	R–Q8	B×P
31	R–KN8+	K–KR4
32	N–N7+	K–KR3
33	N–B5+	K–KR4

etc., and drawn by repetition

Game 3 Tournament 2, Massachusetts State Championship 1967
First win by computer in tournament competition

White — Mac Hack VI   Black-rating 1510

	White	Black
1	P–K4	P–QB4
2	P–Q4	P×P
3	Q×P	N–QB3
4	Q–Q3	N–B3
5	N–QB3	P–KN3
6	N–KB3	P–Q3
7	B–KB4	P–K4
8	B–KN3	P–QR3
9	O–O–O	P–QN4
10	P–QR4	B–R3+
11	K–QN1	P–N5
12	Q×P(Q6)	B–Q2
13	B–KR4	B–N2
14	N–Q5	N×KP
15	N–KB7+	Q×N
16	Q×Q	N–B4
17	Q–Q6	B–KB1
18	Q–Q5	R–B1
19	N×KP	B–K3
20	Q×N!	R×Q
21	R–Q8++	

I consider these games to be an impressive achievement but, as we shall see
in the next chapter, not everyone would agree with me.

3
What computers can't do

3.1 INTRODUCTION

The publication in 1965 of 'Alchemy and artificial intelligence' [1] by Hubert Dreyfus marked the first occasion on which a professional philosopher publicly considered the claims of artificial intelligence. The RAND corporation were the publishers of Dreyfus's work but they played their part reluctantly. In fact they had tried pretty hard to suppress 'Alchemy and artificial intelligence' and gave in only after machinations of Byzantine complexity had failed them.[2] In the event, the article was released as the lowest form of publication possible, no doubt in the hope that it would be ignored. Paper 3244 went on to become the biggest selling publication of its type ever issued by RAND and Dreyfus was so flushed by his success that he felt confident enough to expand his criticisms into *What Computers Can't Do — The Limits of Artificial Intelligence,* which covers the work done in AI up until 1968.

It will be immediately apparent that with titles like 'Alchemy and artificial intelligence' and 'What computers can't do' to his credit Dreyfus is no supporter of artificial intelligence. Indeed, as we shall see, his critiscism of the field is very extensive and not only does he think that artificial intelligence cannot succeed, he thinks that is failure is a reflection of a larger crisis in the philosophical ethos underlying Western thinking.

Drefus was the first philosopher to completely repudiate the claims of artificial intelligence and the first to seriously draw attention to the philosophical problems which AI researchers must face up to; his work and that of John Searle will form the topics of the next two sections and represent some of the severest criticisms of AI made by philosophers.

3.2 THE SOCRATIC METHOD

As far as Dreyfus is concerned, the intellectual roots of AI can be traced back to the discovery by the Greeks of logic and geometry. These discoveries gave rise to the possibility of a calculus of thought and today's generation of computer scientists are merely attempting to bring that possibility to fruition.

The story of artificial intelligence might well begin around 450 BC when (according to Plato) Socrates demands of Euthyphro, a fellow Athenian who, in the name of piety is about to turn in his own father for murder: 'I want to know what is characteristic of piety which makes all actions pious . . . that I might have it to turn to, and to use it as a standard whereby to judge your actions and those of other men'. Socrates is asking Euthyphro for what modern computer theorists would call an 'effective procedure', 'a set of rules which tells us from moment to moment precisely how to behave'. [3]

The story continues with Hobbes's declaration that 'reason . . . is nothing but reckoning . . ., [4] and Leibniz's confidence that he could build a machine which would reduce all thought to the manipulation of numbers if only he had time and money enough to carry out the task [5]. Dreyfus finally brings us up to date with Boole, whose work, Dreyfus claims, left Western man 'ready to begin the calculation' [6] and Turing, who laid the specification for the calculator [7].

The picture that Dreyfus paints of artificial intelligence is one of the culmination of a particular way of thinking about man and reason. With the advent of AI 'the chips . . . were now down on the old Leibnizian bet. The time was ripe to produce the appropriate symbolism and the detailed instructions by means of which the rules could be incorporated into a computer program' [8].

3.2.1   The pattern of failure
When technology finally made it possible to begin AI in earnest, the field broke into a number of subdivisions. Dreyfus identifies four of particular interest: game playing, language translating, problem solving and pattern recognition, each of which he gives a separate treatment. Dreyfus thinks that he has recognized a pattern which unifies AI: in the first place there is dramatic success and predictions of further greater success in the near future, but hard on the heels of triumph come unexpected difficulties and very soon nothing more is heard of the research. Apparent success always ends in utter failure.

In order to illustrate this pattern Dreyfus embarks on a short treatment of game playing.

3.2.2   Algorithms and heuristics
There are, broadly speaking, two sorts of strategy that may be employed in programming a computer to play games. One can program the machine to try all the possible moves in a game one after another until it comes up with the optimum move in any particular situation.

The following represents a strategy for playing noughts and crosses. First find a legal move, i.e. a position in which you can put a cross (say). Evaluate the move—that is, assign it a numerical value between zero (the value for a losing move) and infinity (the value for a winning move). Record the value of that move and repeat the whole procedure with another move. Continue to do this until all the legal moves have been tested. Now play the move with the highest value (if there is more than one move with the highest value play the one that was tested first).

Obviously the interesting part of this program will be the evaluation routine, which in this case will place a fairly low value on moves which put a cross in a position where it has no crosses as neighbours, a higher value for placing a cross alongside another cross and infinity for getting three crosses in a line. Value might be assigned for getting central position in the 'board' for blocking and so on.

If this part of the program is well written the machine will never lose a game and will win quite a few. The strategy I have outlined is called an algorithm and it is suitable for situations where the number of moves and variables to consider (and hence calculations to perform) is relatively small. Any properly written algorithm always finds the best possible move in any situation. If a machine using an algorithmic approach loses a game then there are only two possible explanations: the algorithm might be imperfect (very likely) or the side which the computer is playing might not be capable of forcing a win or a draw and the machine's opponent has played very well.

Another way of approaching games is to program a heuristic approach. The essential feature of this strategy is the utilization of 'rules of thumb' which usually result in an advantage for the machine but need not always do so. Thus part of a heuristic program for chess might specify castling on the king's side of the table somewhere around the tenth move or not advancing one's pawns beyond the fourth rank until the end game. Obviously there are situations where these rules of thumb would result in a move being made which is not the best possible move in the circumstances.

So why use heuristics? There are two reasons, one of which is practical and the other philosophical. First the practical reason: in many games the number of possible moves is too great to allow the machine to use an algorithm, even if the algorithm is known. Some games (like chess and poker) have no known algorithm anyway. The philosophical reason for using heuristics is that it appears that humans approach many problem-solving situations in the same way and according to one way of looking at AI (though not the only one, as we shall see in the next section) the point of doing AI is to shed light on the principles underlying the (human) mind.

Mostly games programs will make use of a mixture of the two strategies above. Heuristics are used to 'prune' the number of moves to be considered — to cut down the number of 'live options' — and an algorithm is applied to the remaining moves.

According to Dreyfus, computers will always lose out when it comes to tasks for which algorithmic programming is not used. It is because the game requires other skills than precise calculation (though of course precision helps) that computers can't play chess.

3.2.3 Computers can't play chess . . .
There has been a tendency in AI literature to overstate the merits of current research and Dreyfus quite rightly takes issue with such over-enthusiasm, using the experience of computer chess as an illustration.

One of the very earliest programs which could make legal chess moves was written by Newell, Shaw and Simon: [9]

> In 1959, Norbert Wiener, escalating the claim that the program was 'good in the opening,' informed the NYU institute of philosophy that 'chess-playing machines as of now will counter the moves of a master game with the moves recognised as right in the text books up to some point in the middle game'. [10]

Dreyfus wryly points out that this was some way short of being a fair description:

> In fact, in its few recorded games, the Newall, Shaw, Simon program played poor but legal chess, and in its last official bout (October 1960) was beaten in 35 moves by a ten year old novice. Fact, however, had ceased to be relevant.
>   While their program was losing its five or six poor games and the myth they had created was holding its own against masters in the middle game — Newell, Shaw and Simon kept quiet. [11]

As if this wasn't bad enough Simon went on to claim in 1962 that the program had played 'highly creative' chess end games 'involving combinations as difficult as any that have been recorded in chess history' [12]. It is difficult to pass much comment on this, not having had access to records of the games, but we might reasonably assume that having played legal chess at all the program could be described as highly creative — at least when compared to the sort of noughts and crosses program I outlined earlier. It does strain credulity though to claim the degree of complexity for its moves which Simon does in the light of its poor results in competition.

On the other hand, Dreyfus was going a bit far in the other direction when he allowed to go unchallenged a widespread interpretation of his view as being that computers could never play chess at all.

3.2.4   . . . But neither can Dreyfus!

As we saw in the previous chapter, one of the first computer programs which could play legal chess was written by Richard Greenblatt and was called Mac Hack [13]. In the light of Dreyfus's comments about the merits of the other programs around it was decided that he would make a worthy opponent for Mac Hack. The resulting game was fairly typical of the sort of thing that goes on between novices in chess clubs everywhere; both players missed fairly obvious winning chances and the end, when it came, was a blood and thunder affair right in the middle of the board. Perhaps it was inevitable that Dreyfus should lose but to his credit he took the defeat well:

> Reality comes limping along behind . . . impressive pronounce-ments. Embarrassed by my exposé of the disparity between their enthusiasm and their results, AI workers finally produced a rea-

sonably competent program. R. Greenblatt's program, called Mac
Hack, did in fact beat the author, a rank amateur, and it has been
entered in several tournaments in which it won a few games. [14]

So it seems that Mac Hack was written just to get at Dreyfus, but whatever
the motivation behind it the program itself is certainly impressive. Chess
programs had moved in a few years from being outplayed by a ten-year-old
novice to beating not only one of the most renowned academics in America
but several more experienced tournament players as well [15]. Hardly an
earth-shattering achievement perhaps but real and substantial progress.
Dreyfus concludes wryly that (at the time of writing) no chess computer has
risen beyond the level of class C amateur. This may not sound much but the
next grade above class A amateur is international master. When one
considers that this standard of excellence was reached in less than twenty
years and that during that time very little effort was actually put into building
a chess-playing machine it becomes very impressive indeed.

Within the last two years one British grand master has lost a game to a
computer and no less a figure than Anatoly Karpov has been in a forced mate
position against a machine — the machine missed it during the game;
however, when set the same position again in a 'weaker' mode it spotted the
right move, suggesting perhaps that it was doing the machine equivalent of
'trying too hard'. The field of computer chess has hardly been reduced to
quiet failure.

3.3 DREYFUS'S STRATEGY

The plan of action which Dreyfus follows is first to argue that there is a
pattern in each of the four main areas of AI research which takes the
researchers from initial success to eventual failure [16]. This is achieved by
breaking the research into four phases and charting the progress of work
done in that area. These phases are as follows:

Phase I   (1957–1962); Cognitive simulation
Phase II   (962–1967): Semantic information processing
Phase III (1967–1972): Manipulating micro-worlds
Phase IV   (1972–1977): Facing the problem of knowledge representation

Having established that this pattern exists, Dreyfus then goes on to explain
why the workers in AI who should be utterly disheartened by their failures
are still 'unqualifiedly optimistic'.

Apprently it is because they firmly believe that 'human intelligent
behaviour is the result of information processing by a digital computer'. This
conviction can be broken down into four assumptions which Dreyfus thinks
AI depends upon: they are the biological assumption, psychological
assumption, epistemological assumption and finally the ontological assump-

tion. Dreyfus identifies the last three of these as philosophical in nature and provides philosophical objections to them.

Having dismissed AI's traditional assumptions Dreyfus goes on to offer some of his own to replace them.

3.3.1   Counter-strategy

I do not propose to spend a lot of time going over Dreyfus's case against practical AI research. The weight of opinion is that his own investigation was unbalanced, if not simply prejudiced. I have already pointed out that research into game playing has not only not stagnated but continues to progress and similar examples could be cited in each of the other fields considered by Dreyfus. There can be little doubt that some of the claims made by workers in AI were hopelessly unrealistic (for example, Herb Simon's 1957 prediction that a computer would be the world chess champion within ten years only provided that it were allowed to contest for the title) and that Dreyfus was right to burst the bubble of their over-confidence. However, the sorts of claims by AI researchers which Dreyfus initially considers are not philosophically interesting and so I do not intend to dwell any longer on them.

Of genuine philosophical interest are the four assumptions which Dreyfus claims underlie AI research, and I will be devoting most of the remainder of this section to a consideration of each of them.

3.4   THE BIOLOGICAL ASSUMPTION

Underpinning AI research is:

> A biological assumption that on some level of operation — usually supposed to be that of the neurons — the brain processes information in discrete operations by way of some biological equivalent of on/off switches. [17]

Dreyfus only spends a little over three pages on the biological assumption — the only one against which he urges no specifically philosophical objections. The main thrust of his argument is that the human brain operates in a way quite distinct from the operation of a digital computer. Consider what Von Neumann has to say on the subject:

> It is to handle all (the brain's) processes by digital methods . . . This is probably how a human designer would at present approach such a problem. The available evidence though scanty and inadequate, rather tends to indicate that the human nervous system uses different principles and procedures. [18]

There are two different sorts of processing techniques which the brain utilizes to perform the vast array of tasks it has to undertake: first there is ordinary digital processing in which a single element carries a specific bit of information, and then there is analogue processing in which continuous physical variables represent the information being processed. Von Neumann has it that while it is evident that neurotransmission involves a nerve impulse . . .

> . . . comparable to a binary digit. Thus a binary element is evidently present but it is evident that this is not the end of the entire story.
>   . . . It is well known that there are various composite functional sequences which have to go through a variety of steps from the original stimulus to the ultimate effect — some of the steps being neural, that is, digital, and others humoral, that is, analogue. [19]

Dreyfus interprets this as a suggestion by Von Neumann that the brain works 'exclusively like an analogue computer' [20]. Certainly such an interpretation does not square with my reading of Von Neumann, who seems to be saying something more along the lines that the brain is a complex computer using two distinct types of processing. But interpretation left aside for a moment I am not sure how it is supposed to make a great deal of difference to AI research anyway.

Suppose the brain did turn out to be an analogue processor or some other sort of processor that no one has dreamed of up till now. The only way such a discovery would make any difference would be if it also turned out that we could not (in principle) simulate its operation using digital techniques. You will recall that Von Neumann thought that we could so simulate the brain's activities using digital programming, it was just that that isn't the way brains do things.

Dreyfus has given no evidence that the biological assumption is actually assumed. This omission takes on greater importance when one realizes that there are good reasons for supposing that such an assumption does not underlie AI research.

In the first place, there is an increasing tendency to utilize analogue and parallel processing techniques in AI research. This sort of research has not been thought of up till now as being not really AI as one might expect if it were undercutting some basic matter of AI principle. On the contrary such techniques are seen as very much the thing of the future.

In the second place it is hard to see how many of the workers in AI would even be interested in how the brain is doing what it does. The biological assumption is surely only of importance to those researchers who are interested in trying to understand the human mind, in other words for workers in cognitive simulation. Now it may well be that such researchers are naive enough to accept the biological assumption but personally I doubt it.

It seems to me to be altogether more likely that if a biological assumption is held at all — and Dreyfus is well short of having shown this — then it is of the following form: the operations of the brain which are not digital have functional equivalents which are. This sort of formulation is in line both with what Von Neumann and others say about brain biology and with the aims of the majority of researchers in AI who are not engaged in some form of cognitive simulation.

3.5   THE PSYCHOLOGICAL ASSUMPTION

Now Dreyfus turns more directly to matters philosophical with his contention that supporting AI is:

> A psychological assumption that the mind can be viewed as a device operating on bits of information according to formal rules. Thus in psychology, the computer serves as a model of the mind as conceived of by empiricists such as Hume (with the bits as atomic impressions) and idealists such as Kant (with the program providing the rules). Both empiricists and idealists have prepared the gound for this model of thinking as data processing — a third person process in which the involvement of the 'processor' plays no essential role. [21]

Dreyfus's treatment of this assumption begins by pointing out an ambiguity in 'information processing'. He agrees readily that the mind takes meaningful data and transforms them into different meaningful data but this is not what Dreyfus thinks is involved in the sort of information processing which workers in AI are interested in. In this sense 'information' is non-semantic. Dreyfus quotes Shannon, who maintains in a paper on the mathematical theory of communication that from an engineering point of view the semantic aspects of communication are irrelevant. Not that this helps Dreyfus much. If we are looking at the mind from an engineering point of view it doesn't matter very much whether the thoughts being had are rational or irrational, reasoned or muddled, meaningful or not; I presume the engineering problem would concern how the information is handled and in the case the specific area and whether the information can be thought of as being dealt with in discrete bits. The psychological assumption does not, as I see it, attempt directly to explain how we get a semantics but concerns itself with how thinking is actually carried on.

Dreyfus's concern is that if information theory is blown into a theory of meaning it has a vocabulary which has 'built in the computer influenced assumption that experience can be analysed into isolable, atomic, alternative choices'. [22] Dreyfus counters this assumption with the Gestaltist claim that 'thinking and perception involve global processes which cannot be understood in terms of a sequence or even a parallel set of discrete operations'. [23]

I am not equipped to settle the question of the value of Gestalt psychology; however, it seems to me that Dreyfus is missing the point in several respects. The psychological assumption, like the biological assumption, is only really of importance to cognitive simulationists who are concerned to try to program computers to do exactly what human beings do. For most researchers, who are involved in trying to program machines to do things which if they were done by human beings would require the exercise of intelligence, the question of what processes humans use to produce their behaviour is at best a side issue. To the bulk of AI workers the psychological assumption simply doesn't arise.

The psychological assumption might be called on to help explain why it is that AI workers think digital computers might be able to reproduce human levels of performance — 'Well, both humans and computers operate on discrete pieces of information' — but as it stands this is both a very small part of the explanation required as well as sounding more as if it concerns biology (the 'engineering' features of the brain) than psychology. In any case, the programs already produced by AI researchers provide enough of an explanation of why they think their line of enquiry is profitable without having to have recourse to the psychological assumption.

Dreyfus next argues that the empirical evidence in favour of the truth of the psychological assumption is insufficient for us to be happy about the methodology of those who subscribe to it. Perhaps so, but more important is that once more Dreyfus has not shown either that the assumption he is concerned about is widely held or it it is so held that there is any importance to be attached to this fact other than that it serves to keep Gestalt psychology away from the prominence it deserves — always assuming of course that the psychological assumption is in fact mistaken as well as being simply unwarranted.

Finally Dreyfus attempts to show that the psychological assumption is held as an *a priori* axiom; he cites the following (from Miller *et al.*) as evidence:

> Any complete description of behaviour should be adequate to serve
> as a set of instructions, that is, it should have the characteristics of a
> plan that could guide the action described. [24]

Dreyfus is quite scathing about this whole idea. He is prepared to admit that it might be possible to give a person some very general rules to enable him to carry out a particular action, but he, tellingly, asks what sort of detailed rules might be given to enable someone to tell circles from squares, or how to tell red from blue. Dreyfus concludes that it is at this point that it becomes unclear 'why or how a complete description in psychology should take the form of a set of instructions' [25]. It seems to me that the reason why it is desirable that psychological descriptions should take the form of a set of instructions is quite straightforward; this method of outlining the description of what is going when a person does such and such a thing is relatively easy to test. All that we have to do is to transfer the instructions to a computer and compare the computer's behaviour and responses with normal human behaviour and responses. There is no such readily available way of testing theories arising out of Gestalt psychology. The question of how a complete description in psychology can take the form of a set of detailed instructions is no more difficult to deal with than the first question. Suppose someone asks me how I can balance a pencil on the end of my nose. It seems to me that I have given a complete description of what is involved if I give the person a full set of instructions which, if followed exactly, enable him to balance a pencil on the end of his nose.

But Dreyfus is interested in more difficult examples than this one. As we have seen, he wants to know what sort of instructions can be given to enable a person to distinguish red from blue. Dreyfus has reasons for believing that it is not possible to provide such a set of instructions. In the first place there is a sense in which people are not following rules when they make distinctions of this sort. Certainly people do not consciously follow rules to help them to tell colours apart — just as planets are not busily solving differential equations to help them calculate their next position in space, though we can calculate that position by assuming that the planets are solving equations. The distinction Dreyfus seems to have in mind is something like the one between behaviour which is rule-following and behaviour which is rule-governed. Dreyfus appears to have the additional worry that behaviour which is deemed to be rule-governed may not in fact be governed by rules at all — that it is observers who invent the rule and that in reality the planet (or person) has nothing to do with rules at all. If this is a worry for Dreyfus, I am not sure there is a lot I can say to relieve him. I have difficulty in understanding what more is wanted of a rule than that it should enable us to explain all past and present behaviour. I don't know what it would be to have a stronger sense of being 'rule-governed' than this that does not fall under 'rule-following', which is to say that is not an example of explicitly following a rule.

3.6   DREYFUS'S DUALISM

As Dreyfus begins to make clear his objections to the psychological assumption it becomes apparent that his thinking is influenced by some form of dualism. Dreyfus acknowledges two genuine levels of description which may be applied to persons:

> On one level, this *a priori* assumption makes sense. Man is an object. The success of modern physical science has assured us that a complete description of the behaviour of a physical object can be expressed in precise laws, which in turn can serve as instructions to a computer, which can then, at least in principle, simulate this behaviour. [26]

We might call this the 'physiological' level of description, and Dreyfus is prepared to admit that it makes sense, although it does not help psychologists much since at this level all psychological terms are excluded. But there is more to the story:

> There is, of course, another level — let us call it phenomenological

— on which it does make sense to talk of human agents, acting, perceiving objects, and so forth. On this level what ones sees are tables, chairs and other people, what one hears are sounds and sometimes words and sentences, and what performs are meaningful actions in a context already charged with meaning. [27]

Dreyfus likes the phenomenological level but it gives no more comfort to psychologists than the physiological level because . . .

. . . here there is no awareness of following instructions or rules; there is no place for a psychological explanation of the sort the cognitive simulationist demands. [28]

The crucial word in this last sentence is 'Awareness'. Dreyfus stands in direct opposition to my view in thinking that because cognitive simulationists ask that psychological descriptions be given in the form of (schema for) computer programs that they are thereby committed to a genuine level of discourse at which the behaviour of persons can be fully explained in terms of their explicitly following rules. As I see it, all the cognitive simulationists need is that human behaviour be rule-governed; there is nothing in their position that requires that machines (or persons) explicitly follow rules all the time; indeed, such a requirement applied to persons sounds more than a little ridiculous.

Not only does there appear to be room at the phenomenological level for a cognitive simulationist's description of human behaviour, the nature of this description goes a long way towards explaining how 'events' at the physiological level can give rise to 'actions' at the phenomenological level. Of course the explanation remains incomplete and perhaps even a little mysterious but computer science suggests a model of mind which moves us toward a solution. Dreyfus sees the attempt to utilize a model of the human brain as a 'computer' operating on discrete bits of information (in the limited sense outlined above) as a sinister attempt to try to introduce a third level of description between the other two and he will have none of it. He takes Neisser to task for saying that 'sensory inputs' lead to experience:

Light waves falling on the retina eventually lead to physical and chemical processes in the brain, but in this sequential sense the light rays and neural processes can never eventually lead to seeing. Seeing is not a chemical process thus it is not the final step in a series of such processes. [29]

The point Dreyfus is trying to make here is that we have direct access to the world. Nothing comes between us and the objects of our experience. In his view, and I suspect in Neisser's view as well, the sense of 'lead to' in which physical processes may be thought to lead to experience is that these processes represent the necessary and sufficient cause of seeing, hearing, etc. But Dreyfus goes way too far in conjecturing from this to our direct access to the objects of our experience. For him 'seeing' is either the whole chain of physical and chemical processes or something entirely different from any part of the chain and in either case 'it is no longer clear why Neisser says we have no immediate access to the perceptual world'. But there is a problem. We know enough about neurophysiology to be able to say with certainty that under certain conditions the whole chain normally associated with 'seeing a pink elephant' can be produced in a person's brain by the administration of drugs; the chain is still there but we do not want to say that the person really sees a pink elephant — that he has immediate access to a pink elephant. We also have good reason to believe that brains do not present the world as it is to us but rather that they enable us to perceive one version of how the world really has all and only the colours that you see and if you have direct access to them.

Does the world contain sounds that human's can't hear — the evidence from watching dogs responding to a dog whistle might suggest that it does. If the world contains features to which we are insensitive and might not contain features which we perceive then what point is there in trying to maintain that we have direct access to the world rather than access through a medium which (sometimes) misrepresents the world to us?

Dreyfus not only thinks that there are two levels of description but also appears to hold the view that not much can be done to bridge the gap between them. I think this strict separation of the level of physical processes and the level of perceptions amounts to a sort of dualism and conclude that Dreyfus is committed to dualism.

3.6.1   Conclusion

In summing up his section on the psychological assumption Dreyfus says that the only legitimate argument for accepting it 'turns on the actual or possible existence' of an intelligent machine:

> The answer to the question whether man can make such a machine must rest on the evidence of work being done. And on the basis of actual achievements and current stagnation, the most plausible answer seems to be, No. [30]

So Dreyfus is firmly, and honestly, pinning his colours to the mast. If AI can come up with the goods then the philosophical assumptions which underpin it, and which Dreyfus thinks represent mainstream Western thinking, can be made good. But otherwise 'the whole self-supporting argument tumbles down like a house of cards'.

The sort of problems which Dreyfus thinks would be the most intractable for AI to solve would be to build a machine which was capable of telling significant facts (data, information and so on) from insignificant facts, and distinguishing the relevant factors in a situation from the irrelevant. Thus it appears that Dreyfus is edging toward posing a 'critical experiment' whereby AI could, if not completely exonerate itself, at least prove that it was on the right track. Later on we will look at the test which was eventually suggested and the reply which the AI community made, but for the moment we will concentrate on the remaining 'assumptions' of AI. It should again be pointed out though that Dreyfus's comments so far have mostly passed right by mainstream AI and been concentrated instead on workers in cognitive simulation. Even with this limited group of researchers in mind Dreyfus seems mostly to have missed his mark. Dreyfus's own apparent commitment to dualism places the worth of many of his criticisms in question.

3.7   THE EPISTEMOLOGICAL ASSUMPTION

The third assumption which Dreyfus turns his attention to is . . .

> An epistemological assumption that all knowledge can be forma-
> lised, that is, whatever can be understood can be expressed in terms
> of logical relations, more exactly in terms of Boolean functions, the
> logical calculus which governs the way bits are related according to
> rules. [31]

Dreyfus thinks that the epistemological assumption is the hallmark of those working in AI (as opposed to cognitive simulationists who are, according to Dreyfus, committed to the psychological assumption) and that this assump-tion amounts to the affirmation that 'all non-arbitrary behaviour can be formalised according to some rules', rules which may then be translated into a computer program by means of which the behaviour can be reproduced.

Dreyfus thinks that the first part of this affirmation is based on a mistaken argument from the success of physical science, while the second part can be criticized on the grounds that 'a theory of competence cannot be a theory of performance' and that, crucially, there cannot be a theory of human performance. This criticism amounts to a reinterpretation of the epistemolo-gical assumption which, far from lending support to AI, actually argues against the possibility of its ever being successful.

3.8   A MISTAKEN ARGUMENT FROM THE SUCCESS OF PHYSICS?

Dreyfus builds on the conclusions he has reached earlier (the majority of which we have seen to be unsupported by good argument) and says that there is still one move open to 'the committed formalist'. Man is still a physical object and since all physical objects are admitted to be subsumable under laws which can be translated into computer programs there is still some hope to believe that laws of human behaviour can be arrived at. It is worth pointing out that unless we accept the arguments which Dreyfus has presented up till now there is no reason to adopt this latest position.

Dreyfus thinks that the formalist's smugness can be accounted for by the following claim:

> In general, by accepting the fundamental assumptions that the

nervous system is a part of the physical world and that all physical processes can be described in a mathematical formalism which can in turn be manipulated by a digital computer one can arrive at the strong claim that the behaviour which results from human 'information processing', whether directly formalisable or not, can always be indirectly reproduced on a digital machine. [32]

But this claim is, in Dreyfus's opinion, misleading for one can only show that 'for any given type of information a digital computer can in principle be programmed to simulate a device which can process that information', and the project of simulating the brain as a physical system is thrown into doubt because of the enormous number of calculations which such a computer program would have to cope with. Indeed, the number of calculations might well be so large that in all practical terms the project would be impossible to carry out even on a computer the size of the planet. What AI needs (and what it is working on) is a system for 'using logical operators to manipulate data representing the world, not for solving physical equations describing physical objects'.

All of this is very well but it doesnt provide even the basis of an argument for the conclusion that the system AI workers need cannot be reached and ultimately that is what Dreyfus must show us. Dreyfus has admitted that human behaviour is in principle reproducible on a digital computer. Even if such reproduction is practically impossible using one method (treating the brain as a physical system and applying physical laws to it) the fact that digital computers are up to the task demanded of them encourages us to look for methods of effecting the desired reproduction more economically. This is what AI tries to do and so far Dreyfus has said nothing which suggests a philosophical argument against the project of AI and much which gives it cause for hope.

3.9 A MISTAKEN ARGUMENT FROM THE SUCCESS OF MODERN LINGUISTICS?

Perhaps the work of people like Chomsky can give some hope to AI . . .

Chomsky and the transformational linguists have found that by abstracting from human performance — the use of particular sentences on particular occasions — they can formalise what remains, that is, the human ability to recognise grammatically well-formed sentences and so reject ill-formed ones. That is they can provide a formal theory of much of linguistic competence. [33]

Dreyfus admits that such a formalization provides justification for half the epistemological assumption, but that is not enough. More than the formalization of the rules of grammar is needed; the requirement now is for a formalization of linguistic performance. Dreyfus concentrates on a 'descriptive objection' to the assertion that such a generalization of syntactic theory is possible:

> . . . not all linguistic behaviour is rulelike. We recognise some linguistic expressions as odd — breaking the rules — and yet we are able to understand them. [34]

Dreyfus follows this up with an example — the sentence, 'The idea is in the pen' raised in the context of a discussion of promising authors [35]. According to Dreyfus this would floor a computer which would, in the unlikely event that it could sort out the ambiguity in 'pen' (playpen, fountain pen and so on), either deny that 'ideas' can be in 'pens' or be forced to make an arbitrary stab at an interpretation. Humans, apparently, wouldn't be troubled by this locution; they would not have to make an arbitrary guess at what is meant. Actually this worried me a little because, like a computer, I was unfamiliar with the expression Dreyfus chose and was unable, without additional clues from Dreyfus, to sort out what the sentence meant. Indeed, I am still not happy with it. I notice that my performance on this test was much like Dreyfus's prediction for computer performance — somewhere between guessing and giving up.

At any rate Dreyfus thinks that this case gets right to the heart of the difficulties facing 'the simulators':

> Programmed behaviour is either arbitrary or strictly rulelike. Therefore, in confronting a new usage a machine must either treat it as a clear case falling under the rules, or take a blind stab. A native speaker feels he has a third alternative. He can recognise the usage as odd, not falling under the rules, and yet he can make sense of it — give it meaning in the context of human life in an apparently nonrulelike and yet non-arbitrary way. [36]

Most of this is pure smokescreen, but lurking within Dreyfus has one very important point. First the smokescreen: many philosophers (myself included) believe that human behaviour is strictly rule-like and that the only alternative to this is that behaviour is arbitrary. Dreyfus himself has admitted that, as physical objects, all our behaviour falls under strict physical rules and is in no way arbitrary. Of course we don't 'feel' bound by rules and there is no reason why we should. Dreyfus has not said anything which is unique to computers.

Grant for a moment that there are (at least in the computer case) just the two alternatives outlined and that computer behaviour is strictly rule-like. What reason is there for accepting that in trying to interpret an unfamiliar locution computers must either classify the new form of words as falling under an existing classification or have to resort to a 'blind stab' at the meaning? Dreyfus seems to think that because the computer is either following rules of behaviour or is behaving arbitrarily that when it comes to linguistic interpetation the computer must either follow the (formalized) rules of grammar or submit to making an arbitrary guess. Dreyfus does not consider the possibility that the computer could make use of other rules — rules which could enable it to make an 'educated' guess at the meaning of unfamiliar terms on the basis of the context in which those terms arise. This is the real third alternative which people have. It is just more smoke to remind us that people 'feel' that they can steer a path between arbitrariness and rule-governed behaviour; their 'feelings' are not any indication of what is or is not the case — people do not 'feel' that all their physical movements are the simple result of the operation of laws of physics; we 'feel' that these movements are the result of desires, intentions and so on.

The important point behind the smoke is that in order to fully cope with a natural language and all its complexities one often has to make recourse to context, and context is often not simply a matter of studying language but usually involves a recognition of the situation in which the language is being used. No amount of reading books of grammar will sort out what is intended when Smith says to Jones — 'Get off!' Even if this occurs in the context of a wider discussion it might be necessary to know that Smith is a football referee and Jones the star striker for the Rovers, or that Smith is a museum attendant and that Jones is a schoolboy who has just climbed onto the museum's Henry Moore. These contexts might become apparent in a long discussion but typically we do not look for 'linguistic' cues for contexts like these when using language but instead rely upon 'social' or 'situational' cues. In demanding that computers stick solely to the rules governing language Dreyfus is building in to his specification of what AI can do the ultimate inability to identify context and therefore the inability to disambiguate as well as humans.

There is no reason for workers in AI to restrict themselves in the way Dreyfus intends, but even if they were to do so they could continue to have high hopes that even within language they could cope with the identification of most contexts. However, it should be reiterated that the only way to fully disambiguate sentences of a natural language is to acquaint yourself with the situation in which the language is being used. It is open to considerable doubt whether a computer which took the form of a black box could ever fully so acquaint itself with human situations. It might be that for computers to ever completely 'understand' language they must be able to respond to non-linguistic cues; in a word, computers might need 'senses' to make sense of language.

Dreyfus cites as an extreme example of the human ability to tolerate departures from the rules of grammar the way in which we can cope with outright errors. No doubt he has in mind both ironic language where one says something that, given the context, is expected to be taken as meaning the opposite of what it purports to say (for example, 'Oh yes, Hitler really loved the Jews!') [37] as well as slips of the tongue and misuses of double negatives and so on.

Dreyfus thinks that one of two situation might prevail. In the first place the computer would have to make mistakes of understanding and be corrected, in which case the computer is never demonstrating the sort of genuine human understanding that AI seeks but only a sort of second-degree understanding. In the second sort of case the computer would have to be given all the rules from the outset — including the metarules concerning how to break the rules and meta-metarules on how to break the metarules and so on. Thus for Dreyfus AI must either accept that computers can never genuinely understand natural language or assert something which involves an infinite regress. Fortunately, this is not the choice which actually faces AI.

To take the first case first. Don't we all know people who have great difficulty in understanding others' use of double negatives, or humourless types who infuriate us by taking an over-literal approach to language? Do we feel inclined to say of these people that they have no understanding of language, or is it more natural to say that they are pedants or (as I have already suggested) that they lack a sense of humour? Of course this does not fully answer Dreyfus, who I am sure would be inclined to say that in reality these people don't 'fully understand' their language and that if AI is to be taken at face value there is no good reason why computers should not be programmed to perform at the highest level of human performance, not at some lower level.

Quite so, Dreyfus has a point, but I did not intend my question to demonstrate the falsity of his position but only to highlight that Dreyfus is involved in nit-picking rather than in pointing to a total inability on the part of computers to fully understand language. At its best, Dreyfus's criticism only makes it clear that computers, so programmed, wouldn't understand language as well as we do, but they would have (limited) understanding. But there is no reason for AI to settle for half a cake here. It has not been shown to be the case that making mistakes and learning from them is indicative of the possession of second-degree understanding. Even if it were true it is by no means clear what significance it would have. Didn't all of us have to learn the subtleties of our language in the same way? For example, when I was a child I thought that when my father passed another car he was 'taking over' the other driver, and when I finally got to grips with this procedure called 'overtaking' I reasoned that if passing on the right was 'overtaking', passing a driver on the left must be an example of 'undertaking'! No one has a complete understanding of English (say); all of us are inclined to the odd mistake or the momentary doubt about how to use our language, so why should computers be judged for making occasional errors more harshly than humans are? The point is that there would come a time when the computer, having made its mistakes and learned from them (probably rather better than we do), would be no more prone to errors in language interpretation than we are. The only danger for AI is one which Dreyfus has not given us any reason to fear — that computers would continually make mistakes and that they would not learn from them.

Now to turn for a moment to the second sort of case which Dreyfus envisions. Obviously it would not be possible to program a computer with all the rules of grammar and the metarules and so on, but surely there is no temptation on the part of workers in AI to adopt an approach even approximating to this in any case. The comments I made above about computers needing to be able to be sensitive to context apply here as well. The most promising strategy to adopt in these circumstances seems to be a combination of rules and metarules combined with some 'sensory' apparatus which might enable the computer to determine context, and finally some element of 'learning' built in so that the computer could profit from its mistakes and the subsequent corrections. I do not intend to minimize the enormity of this task in any way. The program I have just outlined is so far from being completed that it presently represents little more than a flight of fancy; however, it would be asking a lot of AI to move from genesis to completion in just a few generations. No one thinks any the worse of physics because it is not 'finished' or because its completion is not just around the corner. There should likewise be little or no curiosity surrounding the question of why AI hasn't solved all of its problems yet or why it doesn't even know where to begin some of them. At this stage in its development AI is little more than proto-science; it is still exploring the intellectual terrain in which it finds itself, a fact often overlooked because of the rapidity with which it has so far developed. Dreyfus is right to caution against over-enthusiasm but he still has provided no detailed and sustainable reasons for believing that AI is doomed to failure.

As Dreyfus moves toward the conclusion of his chapter on the epistemological assumption he lists a few things which computers can't do:

> (computers) are 'existentially' stupid in that they cannot cope with specific situations. They cannot accept ambiguity and the breaking of rules until the rules for dealing with the deviations have become so specific that the ambiguity has disappeared. [38]

It will go almost without saying that this sort of comment is to AI researchers what a red rag is traditionally supposed to be to a bull. We shall see later how the AI community tried to meet Dreyfus's challenge. For the moment it will suffice to note that Dreyfus has gone a little further towards specifying a set of experiments which might be deemed 'crucial' for AI, which if passed would satisfy Dreyfus at least that the machines involved are doing what his work suggests cannot be done by machines.

3.10   THE ONTOLOGICAL ASSUMPTION

Now that Dreyfus has completed his treatment of the first three underlying assumptions of AI, he is free to turn to the last one:

> Finally, since all information fed into digital computers must be in bits, the computer model of the mind, presupposes that all relevant information about the world, everything essential to the production of intelligent behaviour, must in principle be analyzable as a set of situation-free determinate elements. This is the ontological

assumption, that what there is is a set of facts each logically independent of all the others. [39]

Dreyfus begins with a look at Minsky's introduction to 'Semantic information processing' [40], in which Minsky outlines what he thinks is required for a person to have ordinary common sense, concluding that if a computer which could duplicate this level of performance were to be built it would have to have somewhere in 'the order of a hundred thousand elements of knowledge' [41] and that if it had a million such elements it would be able to demonstrate very great intelligence. Dreyfus's first response to this is to question if this amount of data could be handled effectively (i.e. 'in a reasonable amount of time') but by the middle of the chapter he sounds a little less pessimistic:

> Still, there is work on what are called 'associative memories' and ingenious tricks used in programming such as hash coding, which may in the distant future provide the means of storing and accessing vast bodies of information. [42]

But Dreyfus's main contention in this chapter is that there is more to human performance than the handling of data. In particular, he takes issue with Minsky's notion of a 'situation'. Minsky seems to equate 'situation' with 'physical state' and Dreyfus points out, quite correctly, that the same situation may re-occur without the same physical state being realized. Dreyfus thinks that Minsky is exhibiting a failure to distinguish types from tokens.

> A situation tken can be identical with a physical state token (specified by a point in phase space). But a type of situation cannot be identical to a type of physical state. [43]

Dreyfus's point is well made and he builds on it, returning in rather more detail to his contention that humans make use of context to tell them what situation they are in and hence which facts are the relevant ones. Dreyfus indentifies four areas of human 'information processing' which have 'resisted formalization in terms of heuristic rules'. These elusive areas — fringe consciousness, ambiguity tolerance, essential/inessential discrimination and perspicuous grouping — all make great use of context identification and Dreyfus is convinced that they are not just difficult problems which will be overcome in time but intractable problems which are the result of adherence to the underlying assumptions of AI (assumptions which also, in Dreyfus's view, underlie traditional Western philosophy). In spite of this, or perhaps because of it, Dreyfus is always willing to let AI exonerate itself by producing one or more machines which can function in the difficult areas, provided of course that they do not succeed by getting around the problems but that they tackle them head on.

I am not going to spend much more time on this area because I answered most of Dreyfus's points during the course of the last subsection. But I want to look at just one more Dreyfusian argument before I pass on:

> On the one hand, we have the book: there must always be a broader context; otherwise we have no way to distinguish relevant from irrelevant facts. On the other hand we have the antibook: there must be an ultimate context which requires no interpretation; otherwise there will be an infinite regress of contexts and we can never begin our formalization. [44]

This is a common enough form of argument in Dreyfus's writing; he begins by setting out a dilemma for AI and then presents 'a third possibility' which humans allegedly use to solve the problem. In this case the 'third possibility' is that:

> Instead of a hierarchy of contexts, the present situation is recognised as a continuation or modification of the previous one. Thus we carry over from the immediate past a set of anticipations based on what was relevent and important a moment ago. This carry over gives us certain predispositions as to what is worth noticing. [45]

Of course, Dreyfus is not blind to the fact that, if he is right, this sets a problem — how do we get started? Dreyfus's answer is that we are simply 'wired genetically' to respond in the way we do. Dreyfus does not think this helps AI much since there is no work being carried out devoted to programming initial reflexes and letting machines get on with things. However, Dreyfus is prepared to admit that such a strategy might solve AI's problems even though he is convinced that some questions (how do we develop from fixed responses to our environment to flexible recognition of context?) will remain unanswered.

So again it seems that Dreyfus is not so much arguing against AI as such as against the course of current research. This does not appear to represent a set of philosophical objections to AI as much as a collection of pragmatic complaints about the conduct of some AI workers. And again Dreyfus has hit on an important point without appearing to realize it. This time the relevant point is that in humans there is a stage at which complex linguistic behaviour (the reognition of sentential context) is grounded in biology. There are rules governing our behaviour of which we are conscious and these are joined with a much larger set of rules which govern us but of which we are unconscious, and some of these rules terminate without further possibility of justification in the structure of our brains. Thus it is that there are questions about our behaviour which we can answer in terms of rule following: ' "i" before "e" except after "c" '; other questions which we answer only in terms of motive but which may still be subsumable under (unconscious) rules capable of justification: '. . . the old sentence didn't "look" right'; and finally questions which we cannot fully answer and which may be explained in terms of our physical make-up: 'I don't know "how" I tell "red" from "blue", I simply do it.' The sort of explanation which might be offered in the last case does not amount to a justification for there is no 'justifying a biological feature. The philosophy of language thus terminates in biology.

From the start, Dreyfus has been insensitive to the possibility of a computer parallel to this. He has suggested that all the rules which computers would follow would be 'explicit'. He doesn't make it clear whether he means 'explicit' in the sense of being known by the programmers or in the sense of being 'consciously' followed by the computer (i.e. that would form part of a computer's explanation of why it was doing what it was). I suspect the second alternative is the one Dreyfus is trying to promote. Now Dreyfus is making the mistake of thinking that computers must have an infinite hierarchy of contexts (which, of course, they can't have) if they are to understand language. Dreyfus seems to be unsure of what to say about programming machines to have the computer equivalent of an ultimate context; on the one hand he is, as we have seen, half convinced that it would represent progress, but on the other hand one gets the feeling that he thinks this would represent a way of avoiding the problem rather than facing up to it. I get the impression that Dreyfus thinks (and this is not, on the face of it, a completely unreasonable thought) that programmers should be able to give a better justification for the inclusion of the ultimate context than 'Well, it works!' But in a sense that is explanation enough since we can say nothing better, on behalf of evolution, for our own possession of an ultimate context/set of initial predispositions. Explanations have to end somewhere, and this base stage of programming seems to be a fair place to draw the line since it leaves no more questions about computer mentation unanswered than remain unanswered in the human case.

Of course this assumes that AI would attempt to solve the problem of context identification in the same way that Dreyfus suggests humans solve it. So in a sense this represents the worst case possible for AI; it could happen that other ways of recognizing context might be developed by AI researchers and that the problems Dreyfus worries about might be avoided.

3.10.1   Conclusion

Dreyfus sets out to show that AI depends on four underlying assumptions which both account for the persistent optimism of AI workers faced with continual failure and explain why that failure is unavoidable. Dreyfus has not proven his case.

To begin with, we have noted that while AI is not near completion yet it is not stagnating either. The assumptions which Dreyfus considers are not shared by all the workers in AI — they are not characteristic of the subject — but may be held in some form by some researchers. The biological and psychological assumptions only apply to cognitive simulationists and are not, even on Dreyfus's showing, universally applicable to the whole of AI. Throughout his consideration of AI, Dreyfus exhibits a number of misconceptions about his subject matter; he often appears to have little idea of either the techniques which might be available to AI or to the real underlying beliefs of its advocates. Often he presents AI as facing a choice between unpalatable alternatives and humans as somehow finding a third option which is for some reason closed to AI and which accounts for how humans do what they do and why machines cannot equal us. In each case Dreyfus has either misrepresented the choices open to AI or failed to see how machines might be programmed to adopt the third possibility which Dreyfus claims humans exhibit, and sometimes Dreyfus commits both errors at once. There is a persistent feeling that comes from reading Dreyfus's comments that he has not researched his subject matter with enough care. The sort of laxity that was apparent in his handling of computer chess is manifest throughout the present discussions as well.

However, something positive does come out of Dreyfus's treatment of the assumptions of AI: his readiness to accept the claims of AI if they can be backed up with experimental evidence, i.e. a working computer which does the things which Dreyfus thinks machines can't do. The central claim which Dreyfus appears to be making is that computers can only perform a subset of the tasks which humans can perform and that machines are limited to just those tasks which do not require ambiguities to be sorted out, or which in general demand that the computer be sensitive to context.

Dreyfus moves towards accepting that if a machine could tolerate ambiguity and so on the claims of AI would be realizable. This readiness to put an experimental challenge to AI (and to accept the result!) suggests that perhaps Dreyfus has fewer genuinely philosophical objections to AI than he would like us to believe. If his reservations where strictly philosophical we would expect him to claim (a) that AI could not achieve such and such a task and (b) any apparent performances of the tasks prescribed by (a) could be accounted for, in advance, by the philosophical objections which Dreyfus had already put forward. Thus, despite his combative tone, Dreyfus's case amounts to saying something quite reserved: there are reasons to be pessimistic about the possible future success of AI but there are no proofs around to show that it must fail; AI might yet succeed but it seems unlikely in the circumstances.

I do not think that Dreyfus has given us enough to bear out even this weaker conclusion. He has not shown that the four assumptions which he considers are assumptions of AI as such, nor has he shown that it would represent a serious problem for AI even if it were committed to the assumptions in question. Since he earlier failed to show that AI is dogged by failures and in a state of stagnation, there was very little need to explain those failures anyway.

The most interesting thing to come out of Dreyfus's discussion was the possibility that computers might need to have senses of some sort in order to completely make sense of language. This point is more fully explored by Dreyfus in Chapter 7 of his book and foreshadows the 'robot reply' which some members of the AI community have offered as a possible answer to the criticisms of John Searle. I look in detail at Searles views in the next chapter, so further discussion of them can wait till then.

3.11   THE ROLE OF THE BODY IN INTELLIGENT BEHAVIOUR

In his introduction to Part III of 'What computers can't do', Dreyfus admits that the view he is about to set out 'cannot be presented as an alternative scientific explanation'. The reason for this, according to Dreyfus, is that Western philosophy has decided what is to count as a scientific explanation and it is the very basis of Western philosophy which Dreyfus wishes to call into question and the assumptions of which he wishes to replace. Of course this leaves us in a bit of a dilemma; the methods by which we would normally investigate a theory are those of traditional Western philosophy and the standards by which we judge are from the same source; if Dreyfus is to attempt to overturn this outlook how are we to assess the merit of his case? Usually it would be a damning criticism to say of an explanatory framework that it was unscientific or that it did not provide an explanation, but when its author introduces it by saying that it is both of these and that he is not concerned by this, what are we to say? Are we left with any room in which to criticize Dreyfus's alternative theory?

I have no doubt Dreyfus would say that he is not trying to overturn the whole of Western philosophy but just its characterization of man and mentation. He would argue, I am sure, that most of the methods of investigation which we would want to bring to bear on his theories could continue to be utilized. However, any theory which can tolerate unscientific procedures and non-explanations can hardly be thought as being a mere revision of Western thinking, as such a theory does damage to the very substance of our philosophical tradition.

As the beginning of his counterblast to the underlying assumptions of AI, Dreyfus turns his attention to the role of the body in intelligent behaviour, on which he spends a chapter. This is a slightly misnamed section as Dreyfus actually devotes most of his energy to justifying a Gestaltist attitude toward perception. The conclusion Dreyfus is aiming for is that . . .

> A brain in a bottle or a digital computer might still not be able to respond to new sorts of situations because our ability to be in a situation might depend, not just on the flexibility of our nervous system, but rather on our ability to engage in practical activity. After some attempts to program such a machine, it might become apparent that what distinguished persons from machines, no matter how cleverly constructed, is not a detached universal immaterial soul but an involved situated material body. [46]

This is a somewhat stronger claim than my more limited view that perhaps computers need senses in order to make sense of language. In the case of a human brain in a bottle I would be quite happy to say that it could — given the right input — respond to situations as well as normal human beings do. But would such a brain actually be in a 'situation'? The answer to this is a little long-winded: the brain in a bottle would be in a situation — the situation of being disembodied, etc. — but the situation it would be in would not be the situation which it would think it was in. The 'perceived situation' would be determined by the input available to the brain. Dreyfus would not, I think, argue that with the same input as an embodied brain the disembodied brain would be any less able to respond to its perceived situation than if it were embodied. I suspect that Dreyfus would have reservations about whether it would be possible to actually provide the 'input'; indeed Dreyfus would probably object to talking about 'input' anyway.

My claim is that in order to fully make sense of language it might be necessary for a computer to have at its disposal input which is, as in humans, provided by the senses, and that in order for this input to be had by a computer the machine might need to be equipped with some sort of 'senses'. For Dreyfus, it is not a matter of getting the right input so that processing can take place, it is that there is something about the nature of what it is to be in a situation that requires that one have a body.

Dreyfus notes that computer programming has been at its most successful when dealing with formal languages and abstract logical relations. He thinks it is significant that AI has so far failed to duplicate the sort of intelligence we share with animals, for example, pattern recognition. But, for a number of reasons, this should not come as any surprise. The scale of the two tasks is very different, but more importantly, with the former sort of problem, we are very clear about what it is we are trying to program. Our understanding of the problem makes the programming of a solution much easier than in the second sort of case, where we are still not sure of what questions to ask. The part of our thinking which is entirely conscious is relatively simple to program, but when the processes which lead humans to the solutions of problems become unconscious it becomes harder to simulate human performance on a machine. There is nothing very surprising or significant here. The observation that any task which is well understood may be programmed into a digital computer goes back at least as far as Turing.

3.12 PATTERN RECOGNITION IN HUMANS

> With the aid of concepts borrowed from phenomenology, I shall try to show how pattern recognition requires a certain sort of indeterminate, global anticipation . . .
>
> I shall argue that a body . . . cannot be reproduced by a heuristically programmed digital computer, even one on wheels which can operate manipulators, and that, therefore, by virtue of being embodied, we can perform tasks beyond the capacities of any heuristically programmed robot. [47]

The first thing to notice here is the shift Dreyfus makes from his first reference concerning a computer robot which is 'on wheels and can operate manipulators' to his conclusion which purports to be about 'any heuristically programmed robot' at all. There is every reason to believe that everything that is true about the abilities of the former might not be true about the abilities of the latter.

The essential thrust of Dreyfus's view appears to be that we do not perceive whole scenes, situations, melodies, etc., in terms of their parts but rather perceive the parts in terms of the wholes. The first example we get of this is quite striking. If you were looking at an apple and there were a hazy layer on its surface you would be inclined to say quite different things about the haze depending on whether you thought the apple were made of wax or was just an ordinary apple. In the former case you would think that the haze was dust while in the latter case you would think the haze was moisture. This is an example of our deciding that the 'parts' of our experiences are dependent on what we perceive the whole to be.

Next Dreyfus introduces the notion of a perceptual horizon:

> First there is the basic figure ground phenomenon, necessary for there to be any perception at all; whatever is prominent in our experience and engages our attention appears on a background which remains more or less indeterminate. This background which need never have been made determinate, affects the appearance of what is determinate by letting it appear as a unified bonded figure. [48]

Dreyfus is simply saying that, for most scenes which are before us, our attention is turned to just one part while the remainder of the scene stays almost unnoticed. The background or 'outer horizon' sets the object of our attention in context:

> Similarly our sense of the overall context may organise and direct our perception of the details when we understand a sentence. [49]

However, all of this raises an obvious problem: if wholes are seen in terms of the sum of their parts and parts are seen in terms of the sum of their parts and so on until the process is terminated with some atom of experience, then accounting for how we perceive whole scenes is fairly straightforward; but by what means do we perceive whole scenes/understand whole sentences if Dreyfus's account is right? Apparently everything hinges on our expectations:

> The process can best be noticed when it is breaking down. If you reach for a glass of water and get milk by mistake, on taking a sip your first reaction is total disorientation. You don't taste water but you don't taste milk either. You have a mouthful of what Husserl would call pure sensuous matter or hylectic data and naturally you want to spit it out. Or if you find the right global meaning fast enough, you may recover in time to recognize the milk for what it is. Its other characteristics, whether it is fresh or sour, buttermilk or skimmed milk, will then fall into place. [50]

In the moment of surprise that follows our mistake the reason we think that

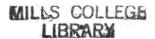

the glass may contain milk rather than petrol is that we are engaged in eating and that gives rise to expectations of eatable or drinkable fare. The idea seems to be that our expectations are organized like an onion; at the heart is an expectation of a glass of cool refreshing water, but if our sensation does not match the expectation we search for an explanation at the next layer. Perhaps the water is lukewarm or is tainted. No? Then we try the next layer — other liquids which might be found in a cafe and so on until we find the right explanation or until we give up and register total confusion.

This is a fairly appealing picture of what goes on in situations of the sort Dreyfus cites. It suggests that by means of our expectations we are able to sift through all the information which is at our disposal in a highly efficient manner. Expectation determine what is relevant in a situation (or indeed what situation we are in). In computer terms an expectation would be a particular strategy for searching a database: first, possible ways for water to taste bad, second, likely cold liquids to be found in a cafe and so on. Different search patterns would be equivalent to different expectations.

None of this gets us any closer to producing a computer program capable of generating new search patterns and sifting data quickly enough to simulate human performance, but it does indicate what sort of form 'expectations' might take if they were to be implemented on digital computers. Dreyfus is sceptical that computers could ever be so programmed but has no new arguments to offer:

> A computer, which must operate on completely determinate data according to strictly defined rules, could at best be programmed to try out a series of hypotheses to see which best fit the fixed data. [51]

Nor has Dreyfus an answer to the question we posed earlier: how do we perceive whole scenes, etc.? He suggests that we use holistic expectations to organize our experience but does not carry his explanation any further. Dreyfus simply reaffirms that 'pattern recognition is a bodily skill':

> These bodily skills enable us not only to recognize objects in each single sense modality but by virtue of the felt equivalence of our exploratory skills we can see and touch the same object. A computer to do the same thing would have to be programmed to make a specific list of the characteristics of a visually analysed object and compare that list to an explicit list of traits recorded by moving tactile receptors over the same object. [52]

To be sure we can combine sense data from different senses to make a fuller examination of an object, that much is not in doubt. But notice that Dreyfus does not provide an argument to show that computers could not do the same. Dreyfus seeks to convince by the combination of loaded language — we see and touch while the computer visually analyses and moves tactile receptors — and pure affirmation. Dreyfus has not shown that computers must make explicit lists, at least not in the philosophically interesting sense of 'explicit' which I discussed earlier. Nor indeed has he shown that computers must make lists of traits in the uninteresting sense either — there may be all sorts of ways of storing data in a memory without making lists of traits.

In summing up, Dreyfus says that the question of whether AI is possible boils down to the question of whether there can be an artificial embodied agent, and that this question in turn is only interesting if we restrict ourselves to asking if it is possible to make such a robot by using a digital computer. Dreyfus is in no doubt that such an agent could be made if we used materials quite like those used in human bodies:

> ... the robot makers ought ... to examine their underlying assumption that no essential difference exists between meat machines and metal machines, between being embodied and controlling movable manipulators. [53]

This foreshadows one of the major points that John Searle makes and I consider Searle's version fully in the next section. For the moment it should be noted that Dreyfus gives no argument to show that there is any important difference between meat and metal as candidate brain materials. If Dreyfus is confident that artificial agents are capable of being made, so long as they are made out of materials very like those which humans are made out of, I can see no *a priori* reason why he should object to metal agents. After all, he is not insisting that artificial agents must use exactly the same stuff as human stuff but is satisfied with closely similar stuff.

It is hard to say what would count as 'closely similar' but in the light of Dreyfus's earlier commitment to experiment I assume the matter could be settled by making an 'agent' out of metal and testing to see if it can do things which machines can't do. If the 'agent' passes the test the material must have been 'closely similar' ('close' here would mean produces effects like those produced by 'person stuff' when used to make an 'agent'). In the light of this and his inability to provide convincing arguments against AI, perhaps it is Dreyfus who should examine his underlying assumption that there is a difference between meat and metal machines.

3.13   A CRITICAL EXPERIMENT

AI is a field which, if properly pursued, brings together representatives of (at least) the three fields of philosophy, psychology and computer science. One of the most unfortunate effects of the acrimonious entry of Hubert Dreyfus into the debate has been a growing wariness between these disciplines. Roger Schank sums it up thus:

> To make matters worse, AI people have to put up with people who state that we are trying to do things which are, in principle, impossible. [54]

Perhaps it is understandable that researchers in AI should demand from the author of a book entitled *What Computers Can't Do* at least one problem which computers could not in principle solve and which would form the basis of a critical experiment. Schank quotes from the newsletter *SIGART* (June 1974):

> Dreyfus accepted McCarthy's challenge at the end to define the 'simplest' problem requiring intelligence that he felt could not be done in principal on a digital computer. He posed the *summarization problem* (originally suggested by Professor Zadeh) as being in this category, even if he wasn't sure this was the 'simplest' such problem. It goes as follows:
>
> Read and summarize in a few sentences a lengthy story (such as might be found in a newspaper or magazine) so that practically anyone would agree that your summary did abstract the important features of the story. [55]

Schank then goes on to outline some of the work going on at his own laboratory at Yale which he thinks will at least set the record straight about what can be done. He reports on the abilities of the following programs; SAM (Script Applier Mechanism), PAM (Plan Applier Mechanism), Talespin, POLITICS and FRUMP (Fast Reading and Understanding Memory Program). Over the next few pages I will look at FRUMP.

What FRUMP does is to skim a newspaper, looking for items which it has an interest in. The program can then produce summaries of selected stories in Russian, Spanish and English.

Consider the following:

INPUT

> A passenger train carrying tourists, including some Americans, collided with a freight train in the rugged Sierra Madre of northern Mexico, killing at least 17 persons and injuring 45, the police reported today.
>
> They said that at least five of the injured were Americans, and there were unofficial reports that one of the dead was from New York City.
>
> Some of the passengers were travel agents, most from Mexico City, making the trip as part of a tourism promotion, the police said.
>
> The American Society of Travel Agents had been meeting in Guadalajara, though it was not known whether any of the group were aboard the train.
>
> One observation car on the railroad to the Pacific tumbled into a 45-foot canyon when the pasenger train smashed into the freight yesterday afternoon near the village of Pittoreal about 20 miles west of Chihuahua City and 200 miles south of the United States border, the police said.
>
> They said that rescue workers were still trying to pry apart the

car's wreckage to reach passengers trapped inside. The rescue squads could not use cutting torches on the wreckage because spilled diesel fuel might ignite, the police reported. [56]

The program produced the following summaries:

RUSSIAN SUMMARY:

V ZHELEZNODOROZHNOI KATASTROFE V MEKSIKE 17 CHELOVEK BYLO UBITO I 45 RANENO.

SPANISH SUMMARY:

HUBO 17 MUERTOS Y 45 HERIDOS CUANDO UN FERRO-CARRIL CHOCO CONTRA UN FERROCARRIL EN MEXICO.

ENGLISH SUMMARY:

17 PEOPLE WERE KILLED AND 45 WERE INJURED WHEN A TRAIN CRASHED INTO A TRAIN IN MEXICO. [57]

Here is another example of FRUMP at work:

A severe earthquake struck northeastern Italy last night, collapsing entire sections of towns northeast of Venice near the Yugoslav border, killing at least 95 persons and injuring at least 1000, the Italian interior ministry reported.

In the city of Udine alone, a government spokesman said they feared at least 200 dead under the debris. The city, on the main railroad between Rome and Vienna, has a population of about 90 000.

The spokesman for the Caribinieri, the paramilitary national police force, said that there had been reports of severe damage from half a dozen towns in the foothills of the Alps, with whole families buried in building collapses. Communication with a number of points in the area were still out.

The earthquake was recorded at 6.3 on the Richter scale, which measures ground motion. In populated areas, a quake registering 4 on that scale can cause moderate damage, a reading of 6 can be severe and a reading of 7 indicates a major earthquake. [58]

FRUMP produced the following summaries:

RUSSIAN SUMMARY:

ZEMLETRY ASENIE SREDNEI SILY PROIZOSHLO V ITA-LII. CILA ZEMLETRY ASENIYA OPREDELENA V 6.3 BALLA PO SHKALE RIKHTERA. PRI ZEMLETRY ASENII 95 CHELOVEK BYLO UBITO I 1000 RANENO.

SPANISH SUMMARY:

HUBO 95 MUERTOS Y 1000 HERIDOS EN UN TERRE-
MOTO FUERTE EN ITALIA. EL TERROMOTO MIDIO 6.3
EN LA ESCALA RICHTER.

ENGLISH SUMMARY:

95 PEOPLE WERE KILLED AND 1000 INJURED IN A
SEVERE EARTHQUAKE THAT STRUCK ITALY. THE
QUAKE REGISTERED 6.3 ON THE RICHTER SCALE. [59]

FRUMP is not a terribly exciting program; its interests and language are
severely limited, but nevertheless it does provide a rebuff to Dreyfus's claim
that no computer could satisfactorily summarize a lengthy story. Effectively
this spelt the end for Dreyfus's claim to plausibility. Since 1978 the baton has
been carried by Professor Johne Searle who, as we shall see, has not yet been
prepared to specify a task which requires intelligence and which cannot in
principle be done by a computer. Instead Searle has preferred to admit that
computers may be capable of doing everything that humans can do (at least
as far as impoartial observers are concerned) but to insist that mere
performance is not enough. What really counts is something we can't
observe directly but must try to establish by means of thought experiments
— whether computers are capable of intentional states.

4

What some computers can't do

4.1 INTRODUCTION

Stemming directly from Alan Turing there is a widespread belief in cognitive science that properly programmed computers can actually be said to understand the world in the way that humans do. This view has, as we have seen, had its detractors but the most eloquent and potentially influential of any to date has been Professor John Searle, who entered the fray in 1980 with his landmark paper 'Minds, brains and programs' [1]. Searle provides a lively and entertaining counter-attack against what he sees as the most substantial contentions of AI and makes a welter of points, many of which I will be considering below.

The paper is built around three main claims: first, Searle maintains that two different sorts of AI can be distinguished, only one of which (strong AI) he wants to take issue with. The second (and principal) claim is that instantiating a program of whatever complexity or sophistication is not enough to give computers a mental life and he provides a thought experiment, by virtue of which the article is primarily remembered, to make his case. Lastly, and perhaps most controversially, Searle insists that cognition is causally dependent on the particular physical stuff out of which humans and perhaps some other species were made.

I will be devoting a full section to each of the main claims in 'Minds, Brains and Programs' and sub-sections to other points.

4.2 A DIFFERENCE OF APPROACH

For some considerable time a distinction has been drawn between two broad approaches to artificial intelligence research. The usual labels for these schools of thought are a cognitive simulation approach and the artificial intelligence approach [2].

According to cognitive simulation the point of doing AI research at all is to throw more light on (the human) mind. Programs are written because they represent a good way of testing theories. Cognitive simulationists strive to produce a complete model of mind, and the proof that this model was accurate would lie in producing a computer program that enabled a machine to exactly recreate human levels of performance across the full range of human ability, with the rider that the machine was also using just the same methods to achieve these performances as humans use. For this strategy to have any chance of success it should be obvious that cognitive simulationists will have to work hand in glove with representatives of other intellectual disciplines, notably psychology and neurophysiology.

Typical of the artificial intelligence approach is a broad lack of concern about how we do the things we do and a greater concentration on what to do. Where cognitive simulation is primarily concerned with human methods the artificial intelligence approach pays most attention to human performances. The aim of this approach is to build machines which can do things which if done by humans would require intelligence [3]. Ideally, researchers would eventually find themselves in a position to build a machine which equals or exceeds human levels of achievement right across the full range of human abilities. Researchers, like Herb Simon, who represent this approach are not particularly concerned to tailor their work in accordance with the insights of psychology or neurophysiology, but that does not mean that they are prepared to ignore these insights either. Human beings represent, in their activities, the best example so far discovered of intelligent behaviour and it would be foolhardy, to say the least, to ignore discoveries about the methods used by humans to produce intelligent behaviour.

Margaret Boden has said that she does not see any basic difference of principle between the two approaches I have outlined and I would tend to agree with her, but that is not to say that they converge [4]. I will follow Boden's convention of using 'artificial intelligence' as a generic term covering both ways of doing AI.

4.2.1 Searle's distinction

Let's turn now to an examination of the twin approaches to artificial intelligence research which John Searle claims to have discerned and which he calls 'strong AI' and 'weak AI' [5].

According to weak AI the principal value of computers in the study of mind is as a powerful tool for the formulation and testing of hypotheses. Searle doesn't actually give any examples of the practice of weak AI but from his description of it we can infer that he has something like Kenneth Colby's work on paranoia in mind [6]. Colby took the information-processing approach to paranoia developed by S. S. Tomkins [7] and translated it into a formal computer program in order to better test it. This form of AI is rather like the cognitive simulation approach in its attitude toward programs. Weak AI is a research strategy which Searle seems to approve of and in 1982, winding up a letter to the editor of the *New York Review of Books*, he went so far as to express his 'enthusiasm for the prospects of weak AI'.

No such fond feelings are anywhere in evidence for the aims and prospects of strong AI. One of Searle's more recent published comments on the subject was:

I believe that strong (as distinct from weak) AI is simply play acting at science and my aim both in my original article and in this letter has been the relentless exposure of its preposterousness. [8]

The view which Searle is setting out to expose is that computers are more than mere tools, that 'minds' are certain sorts of (admittedly very sophisticated) programs and that computers, properly programmed, may be said to have minds.

4.2.2   Can programs be theories?

According to Searle, one of the main contentions of strong AI is that 'programs are not mere tools that enable us to test psycholigical explanations; rather, the programs are themselves the explanations [9]. Searle's terminology seems to be confused here. Explanations or theories are bearers of truth and falsity, indeed the usefulness of a (in this case) psychological explanation lies in its being at least a partially true account of the phenomenon being explained. Programs are made up of truth-valueless instructions and Searle gives no reasons to suppose that a collection of such instructions can act as a bearer of truth or falsity. While Searle is not the only person to choose this way of talking it is still by no means clear what he means when he talks about programs acting as theories. Of course programs might give rise to theories or be written (like PARRY) so as to embody a theory — indeed a single program might easily embody several theories or give rise to more than one theory to explain its operation, and in such cases we would be in a position with machines quite familiar in the human case of having to carry out (psychological) tests to try to settle matters. Marshall (1980) comments that faced with a complex computer program we would be in the business of constructing theories of artificial minds [10]. Searle's characterization of strong AI as taking programs to be explanations is hard to square with strong AI's belief that properly programmed machines have minds, because these twin claims amount to saying that (artificial) minds can be explanations of themselves — or at the very least of other minds. This all amounts to an outlandish view of programs and their function. As Marshall puts it:

> I have noticed that many of my daughter's mental states bear a marked resemblance to my own ... but it would be straining credulity to regard my daughter as 'explaining me', as being a 'theory of me'. [11]

Searle stands over his usage in a reply to Marshall, defending it on the grounds that 'program' is an ambiguous term which sometimes refers to 'the pile of punch cards' but other times (and these are the times Searle is interested in) to a set of statements which may be regarded as constituting theories [12]. Searle does not flesh out this point with an actual example of how a collection of truth-valueless instructions (here construed as statements) might add up to a theory. The following example was suggested by Jack Copeland in conversation. Suppose someone asks for an explanation of how to ride a motorcycle at 100 mph. The reply given is in the form of a set of instructions ... first get on the bike, start the ignition, apply clutch, select first gear, and so on. Isn't that set of instructions a perfectly good explanation? Certainly this is the sort of example which Searle's position gives rise to, but I don't find it very convincing. Faced with this set of instructions I may be well placed to go out and drive a motorcycle at 100 mph but I am not clear that the phenomenon would have been explained, that I would have a theory of driving fast. By analysing the instructions and perhaps even by following them I might well develop a theory but the instructions alone do not seem to do the job.

4.2.3 A peripheral issue?

In his reply to Marshall, Searle describes the dispute over the role of programs in AI as a 'peripheral' issue, but it does not assume a peripheral role either in his original paper or in his additional comments since [13]. Searle has said that he is out to expose as preposterous a certain kind of AI research, and he has characterized this approach largely in terms of its attitude to programs. In the light of this it is hard to see a case for considering the role of programs in strong AI as a peripheral issue. Searle is so convinced of the unimportance of this matter that he was very early on (1980) prepared to shift ground and say that programs are embodiments of theories rather than being theories in their own right [14]. However, far from being a relatively insignificant move in a merely 'verbal' dispute this concession cuts right to the heart of the strong AI/weak AI distinction and leaves us looking for an alternative reading of strong AI. After all, Searle began by presenting the claim that programs are actually explanations as being central to strong AI. If Searle is now prepared to give up this claim then he needs to explain how strong AI can get along without one of its main claims. Indeed, the position is even more serious than this because Searle never develops strong AI much beyond the claim which he is subsequently prepared to abandon.

4.2.4 A philosophical dispute

In fact, having given up the claim that programs are explanations it is doubtful if a rigid distinction between strong AI and weak AI can any longer be maintained. The bare minimum that one expects of a distinction between types of research is that according to the terms of the distinction no one could consistently claim to be an adherent of both sorts of approach. This is not to say that none of the work being done should have application for both approaches, just that the aims of the research strategies should diverge.

Strong AI is now revealed as the claim that properly programmed computers have minds and its aim is presumably to devise and implement such a program. But this is perfectly consistent with the aim of weak AI, which seeks to understand the mind and views programs as a good tool by which to further their aim. There is no reason why someone should not take the view that, while the primary value of programs is as tools in the extension of our knowledge of mind, properly programmed computers would have minds and that it would be a good thing to build up such a machine. In other words strong AI and weak AI do not seem to represent real alternatives.

Indeed, strong AI does not seem to represent a research strategy at all; rather it appears to be a philosophical attitude towards certain sorts of machines. I reject Searle's claim to have uncovered two sorts of AI. There may well be two sorts of AI researcher — one group who believe machines may one day have minds and another who disagree. However, this is plainly not simply a dispute within AI but is part of the philosophy of mind. I will continue to make use of Searle's terminology but I will not use 'strong AI' and 'weak AI' to pick out two sorts of artificial intelligence research but instead to mark a difference of philosophical attitude.

4.2.5   Conclusion
To sum up, there are (at least) two approaches to AI but not the ones that Searle has focused on. According to the artificial intelligence approach the aim of AI is to build machines which can do things which if done by humans would require intelligence, while for cognitive simulationists the (computing) aim is to build a machine which accurately models the human mind. These represent quite different research strategies. Advocates of neither approach are committed in advance to saying that some machines might have minds — this is a philosophical question and is, in a sense, external to the business of doing AI.

4.3   INTRODUCTION
In this section I will examine in some detail Searle's claim that:

> ... no purely formal model will ever be sufficient by itself inten-
> tionality because the formal properties are not themselves constitu-
> tive of intentionality. [15]

This represents the heart of Searle's objection to strong AI and will require careful examination. Searle makes use of a number of arguments to further his view and I will be looking at these individually. I will be devoting a sub-section of exposition and a sub-section of discussion to each of the following: the 'Chinese room' example, the 'hunk of junk' objection and the syntax semantics distinction. In addition I will be considering the 'systems' and 'robot' replies to Searle as well as discussing the role of thought experiments in philosophical discussions.

4.3.1   Searle's strategy
Searle's paper is ostensively about some work done at Yale by Roger Schank and his colleagues [16]. Schank developed a program which enables a computer to make inferences from information it has been explicitly given to information which was merely implicit. Thus we might tell the computer that Smith goes into a restaurant and orders a pizza, but that the pizza was cold and Smith stormed out. Then we could ask the computer 'Did Smith pay his

bill?' and the computer would respond 'No'. This is by any standards as impressive result. To simplify, the program works by incorporating a appropriate 'script' which is a body of background information which it can use to help it with drawing inferences. In this case the computer would have a restaurant script which would in some form contain the information that people who storm out of restaurants having been served unsatisfactory food tend not to pay their bills. Cold pizza might be listed as 'unsatisfactory'. The computer then uses its script and the story we have told it to draw the inferences necessary in order to answer our questions. While certainly impressive, this program should not be over-estimated. Compared with the abilities of an average five-year-old this program is an intellectual dwarf. Sophisticated though it may be it is only scratching the surface of the problems which would be faced by a program which might hope to pass Turing's test.

Searle continually minimizes the complexity of programs which could reproduce the full range of human abilities. In my view (a view which is shared by Hofstadter and Dennett) this minimizing serves to distort Searle's discussion of AI. I can account for Searle's attitude only by assuming either a surprising ignorance of his subject matter or a deliberate ploy by him to make his case seem more plausible than it is. It would be normal to err on the side of generosity and accept that Searle's knowledge of the technicalities of AI is somewhat limited but as I will explain later there may be grounds for taking a less charitable position.

To show that any strong AI assumptions about Schank's work for example, the computer understands the stories we tell it) are misplaced Searle introduces the 'Chinese room' example. Then we are given a page or so of discussion before Searle turns on his critics. He presents a number of possible objections to his position (which we might assume were put to him in discussion before publication) and presents his answers.

A point that strikes one when first reading 'Minds, brains and programs' (and indeed even Searle's more recent printed views) is that Searle disdains to provide conventional arguments against strong AI. By this I mean arguments which begin with one or more premise and which proceed by the usual rules of reasoning to stated conclusions. The bulk of his criticism is given instead in the form of thought experiments or homely analogies.

However, this has not made Searle any less inclined to make substantial claims on behalf of his paper. Recently commenting on the 'Chinese room' example Searle said:

> What this simple argument shows us is that no formal program by itself is sufficient for understanding. [17]

A couple of points arise out of this claim. First, the 'Chinese room' example is just that, an example; it is not an argument though it might be the basis for an argument. Secondly, Searle seems to have re-evaluated the worth of the 'Chinese room' example since the time of its publication, for in the original paper he was only willing to make a more modest (but still fairly impressive) point:

> I have not demonstrated that (the claim that computers might
> exhibit understanding) is false, but it would certainly appear an
> incredible claim in the example. [18]

Such a re-evaluation would be perfectly in order if anything had been added
to the example in between, but Searle has steadfastly stuck with his original
examples which appear in the 1984 Reith lectures in almost the same words
as in the 1980 original version. The effect of this when combined with
Searle's recent higher hopes is to call into question the appropriateness of his
strategy.

While Searle was merely trying to show that strong AI asks us to make
claims for computers which seem incredible in certain cases, his choice of
analogy and thought experiment had its merits. But if his intention was (as
he now seems to be saying) to demonstrate the claims in question to be false,
his way of showing this to be so is at best questionable.

4.3.2   Counter-strategy

Obviously how one goes about answering Searle's objections depends
critically on what kind of objections one takes them to be. If, like Searle, we
see the 'Chinese room' as an argument then the correct response is either to
challenge one or more of the premises on which the argument is based or to
show that one or more of the steps from premises to conclusion(s) is invalid.
This will not be the path I will be following.

It is my view that Searle is not, in 'Minds, brains and programs',
primarily in the business of providing conventional arguments against strong
AI. I see the article as first and foremost a piece of sophistry. I should point
out that as sophistry goes Searle's is very good and the 'Chinese room' does
provide grounds for doubting the worth of strong AI. My intention, in
identifying Searle's objections as sophistry, is not primarily to demean them
but to home in on the right response to them.

Searle spends most of his effort in what Dennett would describe as
pumping intuitions and no amount of counter-argument will fully undo their
effect. I think that the right approach to Searle is, as far as possible, to pump
intuitions in the other direction so as to restore a balance in which reasons
for accepting strong AI may be put forward with some chance of being
accepted.

4.3.3   The role of thought experiments

This brings us to the question of the role of thought experiments in
philosophical discussions. To be sure thought experiments have had an
illustrious past, but there are limits to what they can achieve even in the
hands of such a gifted philosopher as Searle.

The use of thought experiments is fraught with danger and it is a danger
which increases rather than diminishes with the skill of the writer. It is all too
easy to get sucked into the rhetoric of thought experiments. They can be
very powerful instruments of persuasion, having the ability, as they do, to

leave the reader with a very vivid image that is hard to shake off. The more the skill of their author the harder it is to shake oneself free of such snares.

In general, thought experiments should be reserved for the role of supplementary evidence. It is best not to rely on them as one's principal method of putting one's case. Thus one would ideally adduce good reasons for accepting or rejecting a certain position and back these reasons up by asking a reader to carry out one's thought experiment.

Dennett has, quite correctly, called thought experiments intuition pumps, and that way of thinking of them serves to draw one's attention to their real nature. The good thought experiment takes one's, perhaps vague, intuition about a topic and inflates the importance of it by dressing it up in persuasive language. There is no harm in starting one's enquiries by following one's intuition. The danger lies in getting so taken with these intuitions that the investigation ends there. It would not be so bad if our intuitions were reliable, but they quite notoriously are not.

4.3.4 Searle's terminology

Before we get down to the meat of Searle's paper it is worth spending some time talking about his use of terminology. You will recall Searle began by talking about 'intentionality'; he went on to say that the 'Chinese room' example shows that computers are not capable of 'understanding'; on other occasions Searle talks about 'cognition' and 'cognitive states'. It seems quite clear that the conditions which have to be met before a computer, or a man, may properly be said to 'understand' are quite different from the conditions which must be met before it or he may be said to exhibit 'intentionality' or have a 'cognitive state'. As I understand the terminology an intentional state is achieved when a mental state is directed at or about the world. One such mental state would appear to be understanding which one might assume is capable of existing independently of being directed at the world. Yet without addressing fully the consequences of different interpretations of his terminology Searle proceeds for the most part as if 'understanding', 'intentionality' and 'cognition' were synonyms. I will use 'mentation' as a generic term to cover the plethora of mental activities which Searle is interested in. I will, however, when appropriate, restrict myself to comments about particular kinds of mentation (perceiving, willing, etc.), but since AI is not solely interested in any subset of mentation, it seems more useful to generally cast the net as widely as possible.

4.3.5 Searle's litmus test

Searle begins his presentation of the 'Chinese room' example by explaining his motive for choosing to use a thought experiment rather than a conventional argument. He proposes a litmus test for theories of mind:

> One way to test any theory of mind is to ask oneself what it would be like if my mind actually worked on the principles that the theory says all minds work on. [19]

This claim is not backed up with any justification so we can assume that

Searle thinks it fairly obviously true. It is a view which I cannot share. I can see no justification for thinking Searle's test is obviously sound; on the contrary, I can see several reasons why it is likely to be very unreliable. For example, whatever theory of mind turns out to be the right one, our present state of knowledge suggests that it will explain mentation at least partially in terms of electricity moving around the brain. If one tried to apply Searle's litmus test to any such theory the theory would surely fail. The failure is explained in terms of our intuitions about the experiential nature of electricity passing through our heads, which owe more to Hollywood's depiction of treatment carried out in asylums than to reasoned consideration. However hard we might try to imagine what it would be like (experientially) if the theory were true there seems to remain a gap between our expectations (thus generated) and our experience.

There might well be a temptation to say something of the following sort: 'Well of course the theory you mention will pass the test, I can imagine the situation you describe perfectly well. I know that the small amounts of electricity we are talking about don't give any sensation at all and coupled with the fact that brains are not capable of sensory feeling anyway, I wouldn't expect to 'feel' anything out of the ordinary.'

The interesting thing about this response is that it latches on to what is, for Searle's test, the single most important feature of mentation; the process by which it arises is not experientially accessible to us. However mentation comes about, if it is considered from the first-person point of view it isn't 'like' anything and so we are apt to find even the 'right' explanation unsatisfying when examined from this stance. That is the real reason why Searle's test is a non-starter. In asking us to imagine what it would be like (experientially) if such and such a theory were true it tips the balance against the theory. If we trusted to our intuitions, as Searle suggests we should, I suspect we would end up by denying that mentation is the result of any lower-level process at all. I shall return, albeit briefly, to consider Searle's own theory of mind. We will then see if Searle's theory passes the test which he has proposed for all such theories.

4.3.6   The Chinese room

Like all really good thought experiments the 'Chinese room' example is simplicity itself. We are to imagine being locked in a room with some bushel baskets full of Chinese symbols which, since we speak no Chinese, are quite meaningless to us. To this first batch of symbols is added a second together with some rules (in English) which enable us to correlate the two sets of symbols. Finally a third set of symbols is passed to us together with some further rules which tell us how to go about passing back symbols.

The motivation behind this particular arrangement is that the first set of symbols are meant to be the equivalent of the restaurant script in the Schank program, the second set is supposed to be the story the computer is given about the restaurant and the third set is the parallel of the questions the computer is asked and the final saet, which I give back, are meant to be the computers 'answers'. The two sets of rules are meant to be, respectively, the part of the program which enables the computer to correlate the script and the story and the part of the program which enables the computer to answer questions. In this way Searle hopes to get us to play the role of the computer in the Schank program. Searle's aim is to convince us that this will put us into a position where we can apply his litmus test to the theory of mind which strong AI urges because we will be able to say what it is like to be a computer following a program.

Searle is not content to leave matters there for as things stand his comments bear on only one particular program and he has it in mind to play for much bigger stakes:

> Suppose ... that after a while I get so good at following the instrucction for manipulating the Chinese symbols and the pro- grammers get so good at writing the programs that from the external point of view — that is from the point of view of somebody outside the room in which I am locked — my answers are indistinguishable from those of native Chinese speakers. Nobody just looking at my answers can tell that I don't speak a word of Chinese. [20]

So what is the difference between what goes on when I answer questions in English about a man in a restaurant and when I answer questions in Chinese about a man in a restaurant? According to Searle the difference could hardly be greater:

> ... in the Chinese case, unlike the English case, I produce the answers by manipulating uninterpreted formal symbols. As far as the Chinese is concerned, I simply behave like a computer; I perform computational operations on formally specified elements, for the purposes of Chinese, I am simply the instantiation of the computer program. [21]

It is obvious to Searle on the basis of the 'Chinese room' example that no computer in the position he describes could properly be said to understand a single word of Chinese. It is of no consequence to Searle that the computer's answers to questions are every bit as good as those which would be given to similar questions by native Chinese speakers who, we may presume, do understand Chinese.

Nor would such a program explain understanding because the program would be functioning without producing understanding. Searle is prepared to go a good deal further:

> <Computational operations over formally specified elements> are certainly not sufficient conditions, and not the slightest reason has been given to suppose they are necessary conditions or even that they make a significant contribution to understanding. [22]

Searle's case is simple to sum up; we can imagine a situation where a computer is given all that programming can provide without being enabled thereby to understand anything. Therefore the explanation of understanding requires more than the provision of a formal computer program. Strong AI is now revealed as incapable of fulfilment and is therefore no longer a tenable position.

4.3.7 A limited defence of strong AI

There are a number of reasons why we might be reluctant to share Searle's pessimism. Broadly speaking we may divide objections to Searle into two groups. First there are objections concerning the value of the 'Chinese room' example; I have already mentioned the limitations of thought experiments in philosophical arguments and I will shortly consider some other problems.

Secondly, it might be argued that even if the 'Chinese room' example is entirely successful strong AI may yet be salvaged. It is with this, less ambitious, view that I propose to begin my defence of strong AI.

Even if Searle has shown that no computer is capable of understanding solely as the result of performing computational operations over formally specified elements there are still two routes open to strong AI. The first would be to insist that AI is not interested in understanding alone, that mentation is a much more extensive activity than mere understanding and that Searle needs to do much more than he has so far done to undermine strong AI. However, it seems to me that Searle has a ready-made response to this sort of approach. The 'Chinese room' example is easily extendible to cover a good many more sorts of mentation. There is hardly much mileage in insisting that although following programs isn't, of itself, sufficient to allow computers to understand the world it is enough to allow themn to have senses or emotions and in any case strong AI promised a computer which was, with respect to its mental life, just like humans solely as the result of the right programming. If this cannot be realized — even if it were 'merely' understanding which could not be achieved — then strong AI would be a failure.

The second route open to would-be defenders of strong AI would be to say that Searle is going too far when he talks in terms of strong AI's being a failure or being untenable, it is often the case that a wide-ranging area of intellectual enquiry cannot be carried to a completely successful conclusion, but that does not mean we should simply abandon it. There might still be many important things to be learned from following strong AI. It is highly unlikely that physics will ever be completed but no one would seriously suggest that we should stop doing physics as a result. Here again Searle would have no difficulty in dealing with the defender of strong AI. If strong AI cannot succeed then it is perfectly in order that we should abandon it, the field should transform itself. Any other course would be like arguing that we should still continue to do alchemy even though it has been revealed as a pseudo-science. Nor does Searle's claim that, on the basis of the 'Chinese room' example, strong AI is untenable or a failure seem extravagant. Strong AI claims that properly programmed computers can understand the world in the way we do and the 'Chinese room' shows this to be a nonsense, so of course strong AI is a failure.

It is hard to disagree with Searle that, if the 'Chinese room' is successful, strong AI must be given up. It seems to me that a limited defence of strong AI from the 'Chinese room' is not possible. The only way to preserve strong AI is to show that the 'Chinese room' example doesn't show what Searle has said it shows.

It is my intention over the following pages to show that the 'Chinese room' is not a success, that it is deficient in a number of respects and that a version of strong AI is not only tenable but attractive.

4.3.8   What is the Chinese room and who lives there?

It is easy when reading Searle's thought experiment to forget just how inappropriate certain aspects of it are. In the example the room simply acts as a barrier between a homunculus and the outside world. Information is passed (via a dumb waiter?) from the world to the homunculus, who then looks up an instruction sheet or program which tells him what to do with it next. From the outside all we see is a room out of which occasionally come pieces of paper with Chinese symbols written on them. We are tempted to conclude that someone is in the room and that he understands Chinese. In much the same way people were once inclined to look at other people and conclude that there must be something other than physical stuff which accounted for their behaviour and utterances. The situation which Searle is trying to parallel is really quite different from that presented in the 'Chinese room' example. Nothing comes between us and the writer of Chinese symbols. Computers contain in their memory banks all the data they are working on and all the instructions which enable them to carry out the appropriate formal operations. It seems as if in the example it is the room itself which ought to be the equivalent of the computer but it is not the room which carries out the program, it is an intelligent, understanding, thinking sub-system within the room which does this. Although we might initially be tempted to open the computer's case and check if someone is inside there is no need for we are already dealing direct with our correspondent. So there is no pertinent distinction to be drawn between room and homunculus. This does not mean that if we are to carry out a careful inspection we would not be able to account for the linguistic behaviour of the computer as a whole in terms of some subset of its parts. The point is that to look for a homunculus in the computer would be as idle an activity as to look for one inside Searle or Anderson, indeed such an activity is a throwback to the days when mind–body dualism was still widely acceptable.

That we should find a homunculus in Searle's Chinese room is regrettable though not entirely surprising. It is regrettable because it calls the whole example into question, as I will shortly show, and it is not altogether surprising because Searle is trying to characterize strong AI and he is of the opinion that strong Ai is committed to some form of mind–body dualism.

What Sealre's example asks us to do is to imagine ourselves computers and to see if, by doing what computers do, we would be able to understand, as opposed to 'fluently speak', Chinese. There are at least two reasons why we cannot hope to succeed in the task Searle has set. The first reason is the sheer complexity that the task would involve, and I will discuss this in greater detail below. The second reason concerns the homunculus — Searle's demon.

Not to put too fine a point on it Searle's demon is far too powerful for the role which he is supposed to be playing in the example. The demon can understand English, he can follow complex instructions, he can day-dream about the meal he is going to eat when he gets out of the room; in fact Searle's demon has all the abilities which Searle has.

At this point I should like to introduce the notion of a level of description. Take something quite simple like a glass of water. There are various ways we can choose to think of a glass of water: we can think of it as a collection of atoms, as a glass of water or perhaps as a unit of some peculiar currency. Considered as a collection of atoms certain concepts apply to the water which do not apply to it when considered otherwise; we might talk of the velocity of certain atoms or their grouping. As a glass of water we might use concepts like temperature, flavour and so on and has a unit of currency we might introduce concepts concerned with worth or exchange. As the concepts which apply to an object change depending on our description of it we say that the level of description has changed. A level of description can thus be thought of as a set of concepts which may be applied to a given object (or process). It may or may not be the case that the concepts at one level may be perfectly translatable into the concepts of another level without overlap. In this case we are really only dealing with one level of description. If the concepts of level A (after translation) include all the concepts of level B with some remainder, A is a higher level of description than B. The fewer the concepts employed at a particular level the more likely is the level to be low. What is saved on the number of concepts being employed is, however, liable to be lost on the length of the description. Consider what the description of the atomic level of a melon exploding would be like!

Human beings are, at one level, collections of atoms, but it is not at this level that we expect to find understanding or emotion. Of course it may well be (and almost certainly is) that understanding is capable of explanation at the atomic level but such an explanation is not only a long way off but when it is furnished it will be in the form that looks nothing like an account of understanding in the same sort of way that talk about atoms moving rapidly doesn't really look like an account of the nature of heat. We will certainly go on using terms like understanding long after they have been reduced to lower-level descriptions.

Searle's demon tries to occupy a place in the room which is not capable of being occcupied. By being the proper bearer of predicates like 'understands English' (and Searle is not claiming this as a *façon de parler*) the demon appears to be operating at a high level of description but in trying to run the program for Chinese or, more properly, be the instantiation of a program for understanding Chinese the demon appears to be operating at a lower level of description. Of course we will operate at many levels of description at once but it is only possible to talk about us at one level of description at a time. Anyway, in consciously following the program the demon is doing something quite different from what is being done by a computer running a program. The distinction I am trying to draw is something like the distinction between running upstairs without conscious thought and running upstairs while paying attention to every movement. Experientially these two feats are quite different and indeed it often proves impossible to do the latter at all. In the same way, understanding a language is something we all do without thought; if we were to pay attention to the detailed mechanics of what we are doing (supposing of course that we could discover what they were) it is certain that the experience would be quite different and the feat might even prove to be beyond our ability.

If we were to carry out this task it is likely that at the end we would say something like 'It is obvious to me that this process cannot be a complete explanation of how I can understand English becuase I have just duplicated it and didn't increase my understanding at all!' Whatever process(es) we humans use to understand, a natural language or a picture is/are certainly experientially invisible to us and any attempt to consciously undergo the same process will be sure to have a different experiental character.

Now imagine the following case. I am taken into a room and subjected to an operation, data are stored in micro-chips inside my head and a circuit is installed which makes my brain perform certain actions when I am con- fronted with Chinese writing or language in much the same way as it already does when confronted with English writing or language. Afterwards I undergo the same sort of tests as Searle's demon with similar results.

Is it obvious in the case outlined that I would not understand any Chinese? I grant that it is a possibility that I would be staggered to find myself writing Chinese symbols and apparently uttering Chinese words quite involuntarily but it also seems possible that I would simply understand Chinese. Personally I haven't the slightest idea what would be the experien- tial consequences of such an operation and I suspect no one else has either. In the light of this it seems to me that the most prudent course is to reserve judgement. Of itself, the example doesn't show anything very much. Unlike Searle's example this one ensures that the running of the program is carried at the right level without the conscious attention of the person; it is this feature of the example that makes it harder to decide about than in the 'Chinese room' case.

To recap, the 'Chinese room' example is suspect because it draws a distinction between room and occupant in a way strongly suggestive of dualism. The occupant of the room, Searle's demon, is made to attempt to run the program conciously when in fact the program should be run without the conscious knowledge of the demon. The demon himself is far too powerful for the role he is supposed to be playing in the example and it might be pointed out that there is a subliminal pressure on the reader to reject strong AI exerted by the fact that in the Chinese room we have an unquestioned case of understanding which appears to be the result of something other than following a program (who would be running it, another demon?). This lends an air of artificiality to what the demon is doing and in my view is quite prejudicial to the prospects of AI in the example. To answer the question which forms the title of this section the 'Chinese room' is an example and Searle lives there.

4.3.9   Can we carry out Searle's thought experiment?

Earlier I promised to discuss the complexity of the 'Chinese room' example and this might have seemed a little odd since Searle presents his example as being simple and I have agreed with him, describing it as 'simplicity itself'. I cannot speak for Searle but in my case I was drawing attention to the simple structure of the example and the relatively few materials out of which it was constructed. When we come to attempt the test it becomes clear that however simple it might have seemed in theory, in practice it is very difficult indeed.

Here is a little program for calculating the next position to be plotted on a graph:

```
10   INPUT number
20   PLOT RND(6), (number^2)/15.23467
30   GOTO 10
```

The first line instructs the computer to ask the operator for a number. The second tells the computer to plot a point whose x co-ordinate is in the range 1–6 (to be chosen at random) and whose y co-ordinate is the square of the number divided by 15.23467. I invite you to repeat run this program in your head one hundred times. You may care to memorize the program and use some paper and pencils to perform calculations.

If you are like me you would not be absolutely sure you could get all the calculations right first time. Now imagine trying a program of moderate length, say 200 lines. Could you even memorize it? Now imagine a program complex enough to produce behaviour in a computer every bit as sophisticated and rich as any human could produce, which could pass the Turing test for Chinese. I could not say how many tens of thousands of times larger than our three-liner such a program would be. Remember that the program would be the equivalent of writing out the formal specification for a human brain complete with all the information and abilities which the person whose brain it is has gathered over the course of a lifetime. Do you think you would even be able to follow the instructions? Perhaps not, but after all lots of philosophical examples are like that, dealing with matters of logical possibility rather than confining themselves to what average human beings could do. The problem is that it is normally clear when a philosopher is presenting such an example and most examples do not depend on our imagining what the experiential character of carrying out the example would be. Searle's experiment is never presented as something which might be difficult to perform — on the contrary Searl's response to an objection to his position called the 'systems reply' (I will be considering this fully below) is quite straightforward:

Let the individual internalize all the elements of the system. He memorizes the rules in the ledger and the data banks of Chinese symbols and he does all the calculations in his head. [23]

No mention here of difficulty, it's all quite simple — just memorize the entire formal specification of a brain! I repeat, this would not be in any way illegitimate if it were not for the example's total reliance on our imagining what it would be like to do what Searle suggests and concluding that we would not increase our understanding of Chinese thereby. It is the requirement that we imagine what it would be like to carry out the 'Chinese room' experiment that is so injurious to it. Remember also that the person who does the memorizing is supposed to be able to pass a Turing test at the end, so the responses he gives in Chinese must be produced as quickly as those of a native Chinese speaker. Does anyone have the slightest idea what the experiential character of carrying out this test would be? It I am right and Searle's experiment does not enable us to generate reliable intuitions then there is a good case for saying that the experiment is worse than useless for by appearing to settle the issue it is positively misleading.

4.3.10   The systems reply
As I have already mentioned, Searle pays attention in his paper to some possible replies which might be made to him and tries to answer these in advance. The first of these is the systems reply and according to Searle runs as follows:

> While it is true that the individual person who is locked in the room does not understand the story, the fact is that he is merely part of a whole system, and the system does understand the story. The person has a large ledger in front of him in which are written the rules, he has a lot of scratch paper and pencils for doing calculations, he has 'data banks' of sets of Chinese symbols. Now understanding is not being ascribed to the mere individual; rather it is being ascribed to this whole system of which he is a part. [24]

Notice how, in Searle's hands this reply has a slightly fantastic air. As we have seen above Searle goes on to suggest that a person memorizes the rules, does the calculations in his head and in that way encompasses the system:

> All the same, he understands nothing of Chinese, and *a fortiori* neither does the system, because there isn't anything in the system that isn't in him. [25]

Searle confesses to embarassment at giving even this limited reply because to him the systems reply is hardly worth answering because of its implausibility:

> The idea is that while a person doesn't understand Chinese, somehow the conjunction of that person and bits of paper might understand Chinese. It is not easy for me to imagine how someone who was not in the grip of an ideology would find the idea at all plausible. [26]

I shall return to this last couple of sentences in more detail below when I consider a dispute which flared up between Dennett and Searle in the correspondence section of the *New York Review of Books*.

Even with the best will in the world it is hard to conclude that Searle has presented a fair summary of the systems reply. He has latched onto a distorted version of its form and completely ignored its content. A I understand it, the systems reply seeks to explain the existence of understanding in the following sort of way. Understanding is a property of whole persons and is not to be found in legs or elbows or even brains; to think of understanding in those terms is to fall into a category mistake. We do not want to say that Smith's elbow understands Chinese or even that Smith's brain understands Chinese, we want to say what it is natural to say — Smith understands Chinese. Understanding is a concept which applies at the level of description where we are dealing with persons. It may be that understanding is analysable solely in terms of concepts which apply at a lower level of description so that we might talk about chemical transformations in the brain or in term of information processing, but that is beside the point. Such a description would enable us to say that at the level of brains there is information processing (or following of programs) going on but it is still only at the level of persons that it is appropriate to talk about 'understanding'. The systems reply then goes on to explain how someone who was committed to strong AI (for the two positions are quite distinct) might explain why Searle's example appears to show that there is no understanding had by computers even when following the best programs imaginable. Roughly speaking the explanation is that Searle's example encourages us to look for understanding in the wrong place — in one of the sub-systems. Beyond that the defender of strong AI might point out, as I have done, that the sub-system in question is vastly over-subscribed, because, apart from any other considerations, it is capable of understanding (English) by itself which no part of the system is, in reality, capable of doing.

It does not seem to me that the systems reply deserves the off-hand treatment Searle gives it. It does not seem in the least implausible to say that understanding is something which only persons can do and that persons do not have sub-systems within them which are independently capable of understanding. Searle's reply, which amounts to a suggestion that the sub-system swallow the system, does not even recognize the problem which he has been set.

When Searle says that it is implausible to think that if a person doesn't understand Chinese the conjunction of that person and bits of paper might, he is quite right. What he has not done is to take account of what the systems reply has to say which is that the problem with Searle's thought experiment is that it has a person in the room at all; it should have a mere sub-system which is not, by itself, capable of understanding. In Searle's example and in his comments on the systems reply there is only one thing which might conceivably understand Chinese - the man in the room. The other ingredients cannot individually understand anything and their conjunction looks scarcely any better endowed; the man dominates the Chinese room in a way which is quite unlike anything envisaged by advocates of either strong AI or of the systems approach. I conclude that Searle has not only failed to answer the systems reply, he has failed to even appreciate what the problem is.

4.3.11   Dennett and Searle: an exchange

In 1981 Hofstadter and Dennett collected together a number of 'fantasies and reflections on self and soul' in a volume called *The Mind's I*. The book was arranged so that each contribution was followed by some criticism by the editors. Among the papers which appeared was Searle's 'Minds, brains and programs', and Hofstadter and Dennett expressed a number of reservations about it. In the next section I will look at their objections to Searle but for the moment I want to concentrate on an issue which developed out of a book review by Searle of *The Mind's I* which appeared in the *New York Review of Books* for 29th April 1982.

In his review Searle strongly sugggests that *The Mind's I* was aimed at undermining Searle's own views, with 'Mind's brains and programs' warranting the largest individual commentary and many of the other papers bearing directly on it. As if that were not enough, Searle complains the Hofstadter and Dennett went so far as to 'fabricate' a quotation and attribute it to Searle in order to attack him for it. It is true that Searle's paper has attracted much criticism since its publication and that the balance of philosophical opinion has been that his case is not well made, but I should have thought that it was unlikely in the extreme that anyone should have gone to such desperate lengths to discredit Searle. I should point out before I start that Searle's article did not receive the largest single commentary in *The Mind's I*; that honour was reserved for the discussion of Nagel's 'What is it like to be a bat? which was some twenty per cent longer. In any case I would have thought that receiving a lot of attention for one's work was a mark of respect and an admission of its importance. Rather than being annoyed I would have expected Searle to be quietly pleased.

Now to the issue of Dennett and Hofstadter/s alleged 'fabrication'. Instead of having Searle talk about the conjunction of 'that person and bits of paper' they have him (in their commentary but not the article itself) conjoining the person with a 'few slips of paper'. This is certainly unfortunate but not a little careless but in all honesty it doesn't appeart to be a terribly important misquotation. So little does it depart from what I take to be the 'spirit' of what Searle said that I personally didn't notice the misquotation until my third reading and then only because I had come straight from taking notes on the original. 'Bits of paper' and 'slips of paper' seem fairly synonymous so Searle's concern must stem from the word 'few', and Searle is concerned; he accuses Dennett and Hofstadter of making the misquotation the basis of their criticism and of having him say something which 'runs dead opposite' to his original.

Dennett, who replied on behalf of the pair, is frank enough in admitting that Searle was misquoted and that the error was repeated a further four times. But he denies any deliberate intention to deceive — they did not fabricate, they only erred — and insists that in any case their criticism applies

[27]. Subsequent editions of *The Mind's I* appear with the correct quiotation but no other changes are made in the commentary, so there does appear to be some truth in what Dennett says.

Searle is not satisfied that having changed to using the correct quotation Hofstadter and Dennett have any worthwhile criticism left to make:

> . . . I do not agree that the misquotations make no difference to their argument. On the contrary their version of the 'systems reply' makes essential use of the presumed size and complexity of a computer program for understanding Chinese. I really would have been 'blinded' to the 'realities of the situation' if I had thought that the program consisted in 'a few slips of paper' but in fact the statement of the systems reply given by me . . . makes it clear that the program would occupy a very large number of bits of paper which is dead opposite to the view they attribute to me. As Dennett says, 'How important a single word can be!' [28]

Having read the exchange between Dennett and Searle I went back to Searle's original rebuttal of the systems reply to try to sort out where the balance of the argument lay. In 'Minds, brains and programs' Searle first talks about the program being written in a large 'ledger' and about the demon needing 'a lot of scratch paper and pencils' for doing calculations. A few lines later the 'large ledger' has become 'a ledger' and a few lines after that it is transformed into 'bits of paper' [29]. There is no doubt in my mind that Searle is progressively minimizing the scale of the task for the demon as part of an attempt to make clear why he finds the systems reply so implausible. I do not agree with Searle that he makes it clear that a very large number of bits of paper would be involved in a program able to pass the Turing test. At its most massive Searle's program fits in a large ledger which does not begin to take account of the real size of such a program. Searle encourages the reader to think of the absorption of the system by the demon as a fairly straightforward business and it would have run counter to this strategy to emphasize the actual scale of the task being contemplated. When Dennett and Hofstadter have Searle saying 'a few slips of paper' they have merely pushed Searle's slide from a large ledger to the diminutive 'bits' of paper one stage further. That does nothing to correct their mistake but it does seem a bit much for Searle to cry 'foul' in quite such dramatic fashion when one gets the impression that if he had devoted another half page to the systems reply he too would have been talking about a few slips of paper. Far from running dead opposite to Searle's meaning, Hofsatadter and Dennett have continued in the same direction.

A quite natural reaction to this is to throw up one's hands in disbelief that serious philosophers could get involved in such a trivial dispute. However, it illustrates the intensity with which the issues in AI are being discussed and the complete lack of good will that seems to be around. It is doubtful if anyone as passionately convinced of the preposterousness of AI as Searle appears to be is any longer capable of being fair minded. I do not think there is the slightest chance of convincing Searle that a digital computer was actually thinking (rather than merely manipulating symbols) no matter what the evidence was.

4.3.12   Hofstadter, Dennett and Haugeland: a question of scale?

Hofstadter and Dennett (H&D) [30] make it very clear from the outset that their position is 'quite opposed to Searle's' but rather than presenting all their objections they choose to concentrate on the extent to which the 'Chinese room' experiment is performable. They identify Searle's experiment as just one of a family of experiments.

> Each member of the family of thought experiments is defined by a particular choice of 'knob settings' on a thought experiment generator. [31]

H&D see five knobs which might be interesting, although they do not exclude the possibility of someone coming up with others. They control, respectively, the physical stuff out of which the simulation will be constructed, the degree to which the simulation mimics the human brain, the physical size of the simulation, the size and nature of the demon who carries out the simulation and finally the speed at which the demon works. The 'Chinese room' experiment is produced when the generator has the following settings:

Knob 1:   paper and symbols
Knob 2:   concepts and ideas
Knob 3:   room size
Knob 4:   human-sized demon
Knob 5:   one operation every few seconds

In addition H&D want to introduce one more parameter — the point of view from which to look at the experiment:

> Let us add a little colour to this drab experiment and say that the simulated Chinese speaker involved is a woman and that the demons (if animate) are always male. Now we have a choice between the demon's eye view and the system's eye view. Remember that, by hypobook, both the demon and the simulated woman are equally capable of articulating their views on whether or not they are understanding, and on what they are experiencing. Searle is insistent nevertheless that we view this experiment only from the point of view of the demon ... Searle's claim amounts to the notion that that is only one point of view, not two. [32]

There is great intuitive appeal in looking from the demon's point of view according to H&D because the demon is our size and works at about our speed, whereas the 'woman' answers only once a century or so in meaning-less 'squiggles and squoggles' to boot.

H&D ask us to think about another experiment having the following settings:

Knob 1: neurons and chemicals
Knob 2: neural firing level
Knob 3: brain size
Knob 4: eensy-weensy demon
Knob 5: dazzlingly fast

This corresponds to an experiment suggested by John Haugeland in a response to Searle's article. Haugeland wants us to imagine the defective brain of an otherwise normal woman. The brain is no longer able to send neurotransmitters from one neuron to another, this is where the tiny demon comes in. Haugeland's demon 'tickles' neurons in a way functionally equivalent to the more usual arrival at that neuron of a neurotransmitter. Because of its incredible speed the Haugeland demon is able to let the woman function as if there were nothing wrong with her brain. Haugeland asked Searle whether the woman in the example still has intentionality and to the surprise of H&D (if no one else) Searle replied that she did:

> Searle surprises us — he chooses to listen to her this time and to ignore the demon who is cursing us from his tiny vantage point, yelling up to us 'Fools! Don't listen to her! She's merely a puppet whose every action is caused by my tickling and by the program embedded in these many neurons that I zip among.' But Searle does not heed the H-demon's warning cries. He says, 'Her neurons still have the right causal powers; they just need some help from the demon. [33]

H&D wonder if Searle would continue to ignore these cries if the woman's brain were to be the size of a planet and the demon were human-sized, wryly commenting that if the systems reply were appropriate in Haugeland's example it should continue to be so in the modified version. I do not see any reason why Searle should want to identify with the human-sized demon and I am quite sure that he would continue to see the example from the 'woman's' point of view; however, I suspect that this would not worry H&D, who seem to be directing their comments more to supporters of Searle than to Searle himself. The idea behind their comments seems to be to loosen the hold that the 'Chinese room' example seems to exercise over its readers by showing that there are cases in which though it is easier to identify with the demon than with the system of which he is part it is still appropriate to take the system's eye view. I will return to this in a later section when I will consider under what conditions Searle is prepared to see a system from the system's viewpoint.

4.3.13   How do we know thermostats don't have beliefs?

Directly before considering the robot reply Searle rounds on some comments made by John McCarthy [34] to the effect that machines as simple as thermostats can be properly said to have beliefs. Even though McCarthy admits he is trying to provoke a reaction there is a fair bit of evidence in his article that he is more than slightly tempted by this controversial and, frankly, quite silly view. Searle is merciless:

> Think hard for one minute about what would be necessary to establish that that hunk of metal on the wall over there had real beliefs, beliefs with direction of fit, propositional content and conditions of satisfaction; beliefs that had the possibility of being strong beliefs or weak beliefs; nervous anxious or secure beliefs; dogmatic rational or superstitious beliefs; blind faith or hesitant cogitations; any kind of beliefs. The termostat is not a candidate. Neither is stomach, liver, adding machine or telephone. [35]

Let's take Searle at his word and think for a moment about belief. How do I know that Searle has a belief about computers lacking intentionality? Or to put it another way, what did Searle have to do in order for me to be justified in saying that he has such a belief? Well, there was a whole lot of complex behaviour that Searle went through: he wrote an article in which he said he didn't think computers could have intentionality, he had this published, he defended this article as often as he could in discussions, in correspondence, in papers, on television and radio, indeed by every means at his disposal. Of course this is all rather to jump the gun; after all, I begin by assuming that J. R. Searle is the sort of thing that can have beliefs in the first place; after that the behaviour I have called attention to is sufficiently strong to give rise to my assertion that he has the belief in question. In a sense all the work is done by my assumption. So how do I know that Searle is the sort of thing that can believe? To put things crudely, I have to admit thast I don't know for certain that Searle can have beliefs (by the same token I don't even know if there is a Searle at all!) but the hypobook explains the world (or at least as very small part of it) so well and is so completely without evidence to the contrary that I am prepared to accept it without further ado. It would be very tiresome to have to come up with another explanation of Searle's behaviour. Perhaps Searle is not human at all but a tailor's dummy radio-controlled by a group of American businessmen in order to advertise their products, but until there is some evidence for this hypobook there is no reason why anyone should accept it.

Now what must a thermostat do in order for us to be able to say that it has a belief that this room is too cold? Well, according to McCarthy it seems the thermostat only has to turn on a heating system in order to demonstrate the existence of its belief. but this simply won't wash [36]. The problem is that McCarthy has offered as proof of a belief something which is at best only evidence. Thermostats are not on a par with human beings; it might well be enough for McCarthy to turn on the heating to show that McCarthy has a belief that this room is too cold but that is because we have already granted in advance that McCarthy is the sort of thing that can have beliefs, and that indulgence was based on a whole range of complex behaviour which we find is best explained by allowing that McCarthy is a thing that may have beliefs. If the thermostat is to be thought of as having a belief about temperature it must first be established that thermostats can have beliefs at all. Of course it is evidence for the existence of an ability to have beliefs that the thermostats turns on the heating whenever a room falls below a given temperature but that of itself is insufficient to show that the thermostat really might have beliefs. We need a whole lot more.

But what if the thermostat were to suddenly start to speak and said all the things that McCarthy or Searle would say if they were trying to convince us about their acceptance of a certain belief? Perhaps even then we would not be fully convinced; we might require more, may be even much more, but it is clear that what we are looking for (at minimum) is a high level of complex behaviour for which the best explanation is that the thermostat is capable of holding beliefs. As we have seen already Searle is convinced the we have to look for something else as well as the presence of complex behaviour; just what this something else is I will examine further below but for the moment it is enough to note two things: first there is no reason to suppose that thermostats (or typewriters or livers) have or are capable of having beliefs; secondly that, at least in the first instance, what we are looking for is the existence of complex behaviour, behaviour which is totally outside our experience of any thermostat yet encountered. Where we find this sort of behaviour we have at least a *prima facie* case for saying that beliefs (intentional states, feelings or whatever is appropriate for the behaviour in question) are being had.

4.3.14   The robot reply

Perhaps in an attempt to answer Searle's call for more than linguistic behaviour indistinguishable from that of a native Chinese speaker a second reply is offered. It is called the robot reply and runs as follows:

> Suppose we put the computer inside a robot, and this computer would not just take in formal symbols as input and give out formal symbols as output, but rather would actually operate the robot in such a way that the robot does something very much like perceiving, walking, moving about, hammering nails, eating, drinking — anything you like. ...Such a robot would, unlike Schank's computer, havce genuine understanding and other mental states. [37]

This shoud go a considerable way to answer Searle's complaints about the computer's not having any intentionality. If it were not for our ability to go out into the world and pick out objects like 'tree' or 'dog' we would be limited to a Platonic universe made up out of pure generalities or forms. Though it should be noted that Plato maintained that only if such a state of affairs were to obtain would our thinking be able to proceed properly. Thus even if Searle is right and has shown that computer's cannot have intentional states he still has some work to do in order to establish that they are also incapable of thought.

A computer inside a robot would be able to back up its linguistic behaviour 'Some trees are evergreens' with actions 'This is one' <points out a fir tree>. Surely it cannot any longer be maintained that this computer lacks intentionality, which Searle describes thus:

> Intentionality is by definition that feature of certain mental states by which they are directed at or about objects and states of affairs in the world. Thus beliefs, desires and intentions are intentional states; undirected forms of anxiety and depression are not. [38]

How better could a computer (or a man) demonstrate that it (he) was in possession of one or more intentional states than by actually pointing out the objects in the world that it (he) is talking about? One might expect Searle to suggest a critical experiment to the effect that when a computer could not only pass the Turing test for Chinese but could also demonstrate its intentional states as well as any arbitrary human being, then and only then would we admit that it had those intentional states. This would certainly amount to a stiffer test than any machine yet dreamed of could pass. But this is not Searle's strategy; as I have said before, Searle is playing for very big stakes and he wants nothing less than complete victory. He pours scorn on the robot reply:

> ...the answer to the robot reply is that the addition of such 'perceptual' and 'motor' capacities adds nothing by way of under-standing in particular, or intentionality in general. [39]

Searle proposes a new version of the 'Chinese room' example:

> Suppose that instead of the computer inside the robot you put me inside the room ...
>
> ...Suppose, unknown to me some of the Chinese symbols that come from a television attached to the robot and other Chinese symbols that I am giving out move the robot's arms or legs. It is important to emphasise that all I am doing is manipulating formal symbols ...
>
> ... I am receiving 'information' from the robot's 'perceptual' apparatus, and I am giving out 'instructions' to its motor apparatus without knowing either of these facts. [40]

Searle doesn't attempt to expand on this beyond a brief re-affirmation that all he is doing is manipulating formal symbols. Yet surely the robot reply deserves a more lengthy treatment. If the computer is unable to go out and interact with the world in the normal way it might reasonably stand accused of somehow failing to fully understand what it is talking about (at least when it is not talking about universals), much in the same way as someone who is born blind may be thought of as somehow not fully understanding the word 'red'. Searle's objections about a room-bound computer (as far as they bear on intentionality) can be thought of as another way of stating the problem of whether a man who is in fact blind but uses the word 'red' correctly in every situation can be said to actually understand what 'red' means. The answer to this little conundrum lies in keeping an important distinction in mind: the distinction between understanding a word and having an experience. In certain situations and with certain words it is very tempting to blur this distinction and we end up by thinking that in order to understand 'red' one has to be able to have 'red' experiences. But imagine a situation where someone has a brain defect which results in their having different perceptions when faced with any given colour than the rest of us; perrhaps they see all 'reds' as 'blues' or 'greens' (the actual formula doesn't matter, just so long as the spectral shift is consistent throughout the whole colour range).

That person would be quite like a computer as far as colour is concerned. Their language and ours would be perfectly interchangeable; anything they would describe as 'marine blue' so would we; we might even suppose that he had learned to like and dislike the same broad range of colour combinations as the rest of us, so that where we would say that such and such a combination was tasteful he would agree, and so on. Just like the computer this person would pass the Turing test for colour recognition and like the computer (let's suppose) the nature of the perception would be quite different from that usually experienced by human beings.

Is there any sense in which such a person could reasonably be said not to understand the word 'red'? If there is a failure of understanding what is it that the person fails to comprehend? Situations of the sort I have outlined would, I guess, be impossible to detect so I suppose it is possible that in fact such things happen all the time. In that case, if we insist that the person described really doesn't understand his colour vocabulary then it is possible that any one of us might be in the same position. Doesn't this show that something is wrong with insisting on sameness of experience before granting the existence of understanding?

Searle's answer to the robot reply simply compounds all the mistakes he made with the original 'Chinese room' example. He makes the mistake of treating the robot reply as if it could stand without the systems reply. As a result he looks at the robot not as a unit but as a homunculus inside a room inside a shell. To be sure, the homunculus does not directly interact with the outside world but then neither do we. The data which come to us from our eyes and ears is translated in the brain into a series of electrical signals and is dealt with in that form. If the homunculus is blind and deaf and doesn't really understand the world then how does it differ from our brains? Quite frankly I don't know what it would be for us to interact directly with the world, at least not while one insists on looking at persons/robots as a collection of sub-systems rather than as fully integrated wholes.

4.3.15   The brain simulator reply
Next Searle turns to the brain simulator reply, which runs as follows:

Suppose we design a program that . . . simulates the actual sequence of neuron firings at the synapses of the brain of a native Chinese speaker when he understands stories in Chinese and gives answers to them . The machine takes in Chinese stories and questions about them as input, it simulates the formal structure of actual Chinese brains in processing these stories, and it gives out Chinese answers as outputs . . . Now surely in such a case we would have to say that the machine understood the stories; and if we refuse to say that, wouldn't we also have to deny that native Chinese speakers understood the stories? [41]

Searle has two things to say about this: first he comments that it is odd to find supporters of strong AI suggesting an attempt to simulate the working of human brains because strong AI is meant to do away with the need to study neurophysiology, and secondly Searle suggests a third version of the 'Chinese room' example. Now we are to imagine the following:

instead of a monolingual man in a room shuffling symbols we have the man operate an elaborate set of water pipes with valves connecting them. When the man receives the Chinese symbols, he looks up in the program written in English, which valves he has to turn on and off. Each water connection corresponds to a synapse in the Chinese brain, and the whole system is rigged up so that . . . after turning on all the right faucets, the Chinese answers pop out at the output end of the series of pipes. [42]

This third version of the Chinese room does not differ in any significant way from the second one. Instead of simply passing out symbols the homunculus now has to regulate the flow of water in pipes. I take it from this that Searle doesn't see any major difference between the robot reply and the brain simulator reply. Yet it seems to me that each of the replies presented so far suggests a new answer to the question 'What, apart from a formal program, is required to give rise to mentation?' The robot reply offered an enhanced method of demonstrating understanding; the brain simulator reply goes much further by offering to utilize the techniques of weak AI and to build a machine which fully mimics the operation of the human brain. Think for a moment what is on offer. We would be faced with a machine which can carry on conversations in Chinese as well as any native Chinese speaker; in other words, it can talk about everything that humans can talk about just as well as humans can. No one simply listening to the machine would guess that it were not human; not only that but when the covers were lifted and a full examination could be carried out it would be discovered that inside its case there was a precise analogue of the human brain. All the human brain functions would have their equivalent, so not only would the machine be speaking Chinese but it would be doing so using just the same techniques as humans use to speak Chinese. If this is not enough to guarantee mentation it is unlikely that anything will.

According to Searle the brain simulator reply does not significantly advance on the robot reply. I take it from this that Searle is saying he doesn't see any important consequences following from the choice of one technique (mimicking the human brain in a weak AI fashion) rather than another. This is an important confession because it means that in a very real sense Searle is oblivious to what computers do as well as what they say. It seems for Searle computers simply cannot mentate and nothing will convince him otherwise. Searle is not going to make Dreyfus's mistake of proposing one or more critical experiment to settle the issue. Fortunately Searle does not just leave matters like that but goes on to spell out why it doesn't matter what computers do and provides an answer to the question 'What more is needed?' This anwer represents the positive side of Searle's case and I will be considering it fully below.

4.3.16   The combination reply

The combination reply is just what its name suggests: a combination of the systems reply the robot reply and the brain simulator reply. Searle is prepared to admit that if faced with a machine which incorporated the features urged by each of these individual replies it would be 'rational and indeed irresistible to accept the hypobook that the robot had intentionally' [43], but he adds a very important rider ... 'as long as we knew nothing more about it' [44]. Searle goes some way towards taking note of the comments I made earlier about why it is that we are prepared to grant that McCarthy or anyone else is the sort of thing that can have beliefs. Searle has an answer.

> ... the attributions of intentionality that we make to the robot in this example have nothing to do with formal programs. They are based simply on the assumption that if the robot looks and behaves sufficiently like us, then we would suppose, until proven otherwise, that it must have mental states like ours that cause and are expressed by its behaviour ... If we knew independently how to account for its behavior without such assumptions we would not attribute intentionality to it, especially if we knew it had a formal program. [45]

I am not absolutely clear as to whether Searle is saying that the discovery of the existence of a formal program is sufficient by itself to rule out any possible ascriptions of intentionality or if we need further proof. I am tempted by the former view since it fits best with Searle's general scepticism about computer mentation; however, I am reluctant to ascribe this view to Searle because it runs him straight into trouble. Searle goes on to say that human beings are 'the instantiation of any number of computer programs' and if we ascribe the radical view above to him it would follow that Searle believes that ascriptions of intentionality to humans are misplaced, clearly the opposite of Searle's opinion. On the other hand, if we need independent proof that computers do not mentate Searle has yet to provide it. Of course Searle would say that the 'Chinese room' experiment is proof that computers do not mentate, but in the light of the arguments I have put forward against the 'Chinese room' experiment this would seem to be a very contentious claim indeed.

4.3.17   The 'other minds' reply

Searle now turns to the 'other minds' reply, which runs as follows:

> How do you know that other people understand Chinese or any-
> thing else? Only by their behavior. Now the computer can pass the
> behavioral tests as well as they can (in principle), so if you are going
> to attribute cognition to other people you must in principle also
> attribute it to computers. [46]

Searle thinks that this response is 'only worth a short reply' [47] and says that
it is indicative of a misunderstanding of his case. The problem, he reminds
us, is not one of knowing when it is appropriate to make attributions of
consciousness: it is a question of fully appreciating the nature of what is
being attributed. The force of Searle's comments are, however, much
diminished by his failure to come up with good reasons for believing that the
sort of complex computer behaviour outlined above is possible in the
absence of mentation. What the 'other minds' reply is saying is that unless
there are good reasons to believe otherwise we are justified in attributing
mentation to anything that behaves in certain complex ways. The 'other
minds' advocates are not in a y doubt about the nature of what is being
attributed when they attribute mentation. However, it seems odd to me that
Searle should be so apparently unconcerned about the conditions under
which such ascriptions can properly be made.

4.3.18   The 'many mansions' reply

The 'many mansions' reply stresses the possibility of technological progress
for AI and goes as follows:

> Your whole argument presupposes that AI is only about analogue
> and digital computers. But that just happens to be the present state
> of technology ... your arguments are in no way directed at the
> ability of artificial intelligence to produce and explain cognition.
> [48]

Again Searle settles for a very short response, this time to the effect that the
'many mansions' reply 'trivialises the project of strong AI by redefining it as
whatever artificially produces and explains cognition'. This need not give
rise to an undue amount of concern for defenders of AI because as we saw
earlier strong AI is Searle's invention and does not represent an actual
research position but a philosophical attitude towards that research. AI, as
such, is only concerned to build machines which can do things which if done
by us would require intelligence or which accurately model the operation of
the (human) mind. However, the 'many mansions' reply does not get us very
much further if we want to defend strong AI, but on the other hand I don't
think it is fair to say that the project of strong AI is being trivialized. The
important thing for strong AI, as presented by Searle, is that mentation
results from programming and thus it is hardly to depart far from strong AI

to remind us that machines which might pass the Turing test will be using very different engineering and/or programming techniques than those around today.

4.3.19 Conclusion
We have seen Searle present and attempt to defend from attack the principal weapon in his armoury — the 'Chinese room' example. The example was presented as a way of calling into question some of the recent work done at Yale by Roger Schank and his colleagues, but in Searle's hands it becomes much more. Searle wants to call into question the whole project of strong AI. He wants to show up as preposterous any claim that computers following formal programs might mentate like ordinary human beings.

The 'Chinese room' example has been revealed as inadequate for Searle's purposes. The role of the homunculus has been demonstrated to be of particular concern, and nothing that Searle added to the example in order to deal with the robot or brain simulator replies does anything to remove its basic weakness.

We have seen Searle present his view that no matter how impressive the achievement of programmers might become, no matter what machines might be able to do (or appear to be able to do), they cannot mentate. Computers might even have a one to one correspondence between computation states and human brain states but even that would not produce any mental activity in them. Searle's constant position has been that formal programs are quite simply not enough, machines need something else if they are ever to mentate. As I indicated in my introduction to Searle's work the thing that we have and computers lack is the actual physical stuff out of which humans are made. In the next chapter I will be considering Searle's theory of mind and its close cousin, the 'hunk of junk' objection to strong AI.

4.4 INTRODUCTION

In this section I will be considering in detail two closely related aspects of Searle's case.

First I will be discussing the so-called 'hunk of junk' objection to strong ASI which insists that certain sorts of physical material are not appropriate for supporting mentation. Secondly I will be discussing the positive content of 'Minds, brains and programs' namely Searle's contention that only physical stuff which has the same causal powers as the stuff out of which humans are made can give rise to mentation.

For the remainder of this section I will be turning my attention to three other important questions arising out of Searle's article. First, I will deal with Searle's views on the syntax/semantics distinction. Secondly, I will be considering whether strong AI can be thought of as creating intelligent systems as opposed to merely simulating intelligence. Lastly, I will be examining the extent to which strong AI relies on some form of residual dualism.

4.4.1   The 'hunk of junk' objection

Searle first raises the hunk of junk objection as part of an attempt to show how the equation 'mind is to brain as program is to hardware' breaks down.

> First, the distinction between program and realization has the consequence that the same program could have all sorts of crazy realizations that had no form of intentionality. Weizenbaum (1976, Ch. 2), for example, shows in detail how to construct a computer using a roll of toilet paper and pile of small stones. Similarly the Chinese story-understanding program can be programmed into a sequence of water pipes, a set of wind machines, or a monolingual English speaker, none of which thereby acquires an understanding of Chinese. Stones, toilet paper, wind and water pipes are the wrong kind of stuff to have intentionality in the first place — only something that has the same causal powers as brains can have intentionality — and though the English speaker has the right kind of stuff for intentionality you can easily see that he doesn't get any extra intentionality by memorizing the program since memorizing it won't teach him Chinese. [49]

The most important thing to notice about this is the way in which Searle uses the Chinese room and the hunk of junk objection together to attempt to defeat the claims of strong AI. It seems that there are two important elements in acquiring the ability to mentate. First one must be made from the right stuff but secondly and of equal importance one must be behaving in the right way. Thus it isn't enough simply to memorize a program since that won't enable you to understand Chinese. There seems to be an attempt on Searle's part to use the Chinese room example and the hunk of junk objection as a single weapon against strong AI rather than as two separate weapons.

But I wonder what Searle's response would be if faced with the following example? Suppose I don't try to get a monolingual English speaker to memorize the program for understanding Chinese, but instead 'wire and program' into him. I mean by this that I perform an operation on his brain that makes it behave just like a native Chinese speaker's brain when faced with Chinese symbols or sounds. Of course the output would be no different in the 'wired in' case than in the case where the man has simply memorized the program but clearly the inner activity would be different. In the 'wired in' case the man would not be 'consciously' following a program but would simply be doing what the program indicated he should do (as if by instinct). If the 'wired in' man still doesn't really understand Chinese then I despair of his ever understanding another language. After all what more can the poor creature do? His responses and pronunciation are as good as anything a native Chinese speaker could produce and not only that but he is made of what Searle would have us believe is the 'right stuff' for understanding Chinese (or anything else) and his brain is doing exactly what native Chinese speakers brains do in similar circumstances. Is there anything more that can be demanded?

On the other hand it doesn't help Searle's case much to say that the man does now understand Chinese because if he does so there doesn't seem to be any good way of avoiding the claim that he does so by virtue of the program for understanding Chinese which he is still following (though not consciously so) and the Chinese room example was supposed to have shown us that increased understanding could not be the result of merely following a program.

Perhaps the Chinese room example only applies to those cases where the 'thing' following the program is unfortunate enough to be fashioned out of the wrong stuff. If so, Searle may be able to retrieve matters.

What Searle needs to do in this situation is to compile a list of proscribed materials; he has already told us what to look out for — materials which do not have the same causal powers as brains. It appears that the list will, include such exotic materials as toilet paper, wind and water pipes (though curiously not blood pipes like veins and arteries) and piles of small stones.

Unfortunately Searle never makes it clear why he is so sure that toilet paper and stones cannot support intentionality. I can think of just two reasons why Searle might be so convinced but I hesitate to attribute either to him since they are unworthy of any philosopher much less one of the best philosophers living. It might be that the idea of cogitating toilet paper just strikes Searle as a silly idea but one would hardly expect a philospher to be put off an idea just because it doesn't sound likely.

On the other hand, it might be that Searle is again making the mistake of not clearly distinguishing between levels of description. In this case there are various levels at which we might describe 'stuff'. Imagine two containers each of which is divided into two sections. The first container has hydrogen in one section and oxygen in the other, while the second container has both of its sections filled with water. At one level of description the containers can be thought of as containing the very same stuff in that (let's suppose) they each have exactly the same number of hydrogen and oxygen molecules, but at another level of description the containers could not contain stuffs which are more dissimilar, after all one container is filled with gases while the other contains a liquid. The change in levels is marked by a willingness or unwillingness to take the organizational structure of the groups of molecules into account. In the same way brain stuff (viewed as molecules) might be possibly be reorganized in such a way as to form some toilet paper and stones.

Of course Searle has a ready-made (and perfectly acceptable) answer to this. Water has quite different properties from hydrogen and oxygen: most people would prefer the local fire brigade to put water on their burning house than hydrogen and oxygen. So while brain stuff might take all sorts of strange guises it is only when organized as brain stuff that it can support intentionality. I am quite prepared to go along with this sort of reply but it is not the end of the story by any means. Suppose for sake of simplicity that the stuff brains are made out of is simply complex forms of two sorts of atom, A and B. Now imagine that instead of being atom-sized the atoms were respectively the size of a roll of toilet paper and a small stone. There is no reason to suppose that this would in any way impair the structure's ability to support intentionality. Now if it were possible to somehow duplicate the precise organization of the A and B atoms using rolls of toilet paper and small stones then there is every reason to suppose that the resulting structure would also be able to support consciousness. If this seems odd then consider the implications of its denial, the only remaining explanation for the brain's ability to support intentionality (or any sort of mentation) would have to be located in some characteristic of the A and B atoms themselves — a feature which is made manifest by the complex structure of which each atom is a part. To date, we are totally ignorant of any such 'mentation supporting characteristic in any of the atoms which make up the brain. Since we have not been able to discover such a characteristic what reason do we have for believing that it exists at all? Only that we see evidence of mentation all around us. The evidence is in the form of complex behaviour and that evidence would be equally good if it occurred in toilet paper and stones as it is when it occurs in humans. However Searle remains unconvinced;

> So let us imagine (a thirst-simulating program) running on a computer made entirely of old beer cans, millions (or billions) of old beer cans that are rigged up to levers and powered by windmills. We can imagine that the program simulates the neuron firings at the synapses of having beer cans bang into each other, thus achieving a strict correspondence between neuron firings and beer can bangings. And at the end of the sequence a beer can pops up on which is written 'I am thirsty.' Now. . .does anyone suppose that this Rube Goldberg apparatus is literally thirsty in the sense in which you and I are? [50]

Notice how Searle uses all his resources to make this example seem as incredible as possible. He chooses not just beer cans but 'old beer cans' suggesting uselessness. The power source is courtesy of some archaic windmill device and a collection of levers. The whole setup is described as a 'Rube Goldberg apparatus', hardly a description to inspire much confidence. This sluggish and eccentric beer can banging apparatus to be compared with the operation of the human brain. I must make it clear that I do not object to Searle's choice of materials out of which to make the machine I am only pointing to the way in which the wording of the example serves to distract us from a dispassionate consideration of the machine's merits.

However there is one place in this example where Searle doesn't fight fair; it is where he describes the output of the device. Forget the rest of the example for a moment and ask yourself would some letters on a beer can convince you that the machine out of which it came was thirsty? More importantly, does writing something on an old beer can amount to behaviour which would constitute a pass of the Turing test for 'thirst'? Clearly the output of this machine is never going to convince; such a way of communicating with us would prevent the machine ever passing the Turing test for 'thirst'. Searle is supposed to be demonstrating that a machine which combines the features put forward in the systems, robot and brain simulators replies but which was made out of material greatly different from human brain stuff could not (notice 'could not') mentate. The Rube Godlberg apparatus never comes near to meeting that challenge. Either it should be compared with a brain on the same scale planet-sized) or it should have been made smaller, but in any case the end result should have been behaving quite differently; it should have been duplicating all the behaviour of a thirsty human. Would it be quite so easy to dismiss a (microscopic) beer can machine which begged and pleaded for a drink and if we could ignore its cries how would we react when it eventually lay down and 'ceased to function'. Would it be quite so easy to maintain as Cartesians once did of other animals that it felt nothing or that it wasn't really thirsty at all? Of course the cartesian example (and many others) show that it is possible for us to hold Searle's view, but is it really as obvious (or attractive) as he makes it sound?

Of course it is easy to get the idea that toilet paper and stones can't mentate because we are so used to them not giving any evidence of mentation. It would conme as something of a surprise to suddenly find oneself in conversation with a roll of toilet paper indeed there is something more than faintly absurd about the suggestion that such a conversation might happen. But by the same token there is something more than a little absurd about the suggestion that one might find oneself in conversation with some amino acid or a passing spiral of DNA.

Just as there is a world of difference between saying that A and B atoms can mentate and saying that there might be mentating structure built out of A and B atoms, there is a huge difference between saying that toilet roll can mentate and saying that it might be possible to build a mentating machine out of toilet rolls.

Searle has stuck with the hunk of junk objection right up to the present day — it is to be found in the 1948 Reith Lectures and in Searle's contribution to the *New York Review of Books* — but I can see nothing in the objection to justify Searle's confidence in it. I have showed in this subsection that there is at least a *prima facie* case for not disqualifying any material out of hand. Combined with my arguments against the Chinese room example I think that the substance of Searle's negative position (his attempt to show the preposterousness of strong AI) is in tatters.

4.4.2   The causal powers of the brain

Now we may turn to Searle's positive book about the nature of mentation:

> It is not because I am the instantiation of a computer program that I am able to understand English and have other forms of intentionality (I am, I suppose the instantiation of any number of computer programs) but as far as we know it is because I am a certain sort of organism with a certain biological (i.e. chemical and physical) structure and this structure, under certain conditions, is causally capable of producing perception, action, understanding, learning

and other intentional phenomenons. And the point of the present argument is that only something that had those causal powers could have that intentionality. [51]

There are in fact two planks to Searle's positive case: the first, as we have seen, is the contention that only certain sorts of stuff can support intentionality and that intentionality is to be explained in terms of the stuff out of which the intentional system is constructed and the second plank is that deciding which sorts of stuff have the right causal powers to produce intentionality is an empirical matter.

Perhaps other physical and chemical processes could produce exactly these effects; perhaps for example Martians also have intentionality but their brains are made of different stuff. That is an empirical question rather like the question whether photosynbook can be done with a chemistry different from that of chlorophyll. [52]

Searle goes to some lengths to stress both these points over and over again. He tells us that:

What matters about brain operations is not the formal shadow cast by the sequence of synapses but rather the actual properties of the sequences. [53]

Strong AI goes wrong by claiming that 'the shadows are the real thing'. It seems that in spite of himself Searle is in danger of proposing a critical experiment. He repeatedly says that discovering whether a certain sort of stuff can cause mentation is like checking to see if photosynbook or lactation can be carried out by different methods than are usually employed. This makes it sound as if Searle thinks we should be looking for a substance which the brain produces and which other substances that cannot cause mentation do not produce. I am quite sure that Searle does not intend to promote any such theory but if it is an empirical matter whether a certain sort of stuff can mentate then there should be some experiment we can carry out in order to establish for sure if a machine is mentating.

Perhaps Searle has a test in mind; he may even have already applied it to rolls of toilet paper, to small stones, and to wind and water pipes; old beer cans and levers may already have failed Searle's test but if so Searle isn't telling. Curiously enough Searle doesn't even hint at what such a test might look like (or what it might be looking for). Searle's reluctance is particularly unfortunate because of an incident which I am now able to reveal for the first time.

For reasons of national security it has never been widely known that some years ago a spaceship crash-landed just outside Belfast. The authorities, who had been closely following the movements of the craft, were quickly on the scene and were as a result able to recover one of the crew in apparent good health.

The creature was, of course, subjected to extensive tests, but took the examinations in very good part keeping the team amused with a series of moonman jokes. The investigation revealed much about extra-terrestrial biology. The creature was discovered to be just about as unlike us as it is possible to be.

An area of particular interest was the alien's neurophysiology. It was found that he(?) had a geletinous green mass in the middle of his body which appeared to carry out the family of tasks attended to in humans by the brain. With great care and attention the processes by which this alien brain operated were uncovered. It was no surprise after the team's earlier findings to discover that alien brains work on different principles from ours. Still, the principles were considered such that like us the alien could be regarded as the instantiation of a number of (as yet unwritten) computer programs.

The physical tests over, a team of psychiatrists moved in and began their investigation. But their report, when it finally appeared, was called into question by a group of sceptical philosophers. The problem was simple. According to the philosophers, there was, as yet, no concrete evidence to suggest that the alien was conscious, much less well balanced and happy — protests from the alien were ruled out of order at this point. The balance of philosophical opinion was that humans are conscious not by virtue of instantiating any number of computer programs nor yet by virtue of their being able to behave in certain specifiable ways (answering questions correctly, acting appropriately in given circumstances, etc.) but by virtue of the causal power of their brains. So deciding if the creature was conscious or if he understood what was said to him was a matter of determining the causal power of the creature's brain. Of course this was an empirical investigation and could be safely left to the scientists.

The team of scientists was none to happy with the situation. The philosophers had set them a task which posed a methodological problem: how do you establish that two brains have the same causal powers? It being tea time, the team were already thinking about water and it occurred to them that there are various ways in which water can be made. For example you can begin with some H_3O and chemically strip off a hydrogen atom or start with some HO and chemically add a hydrogen atom. Now there could be no two processes which could be more different (being opposites after all) but with regard to producing water they could be thought of as causally equivalent. How could we be sure they really were equivalent? That was easy, all that was needed was to test the end product in each case, if it turned out to be pure H_2O the processes were causally equivalent, otherwise not.

Similar examples were generated covering milk and biscuits but it soon become apparent that the team had a new methodological problem and that this one could not be solved in a tea break. How could one test for the presence of mentation? The team had already established beyond doubt that the alien was the instantiation of many formal programs and that he was possessed of the ability to answer questions about a wide range of subjects up to human levels of performance, his grasp of interstellar navigation left everyone breathless, he seemed to have picked up English rather well, and since this latest row with the philosophers he had taken to tragic poetry with a flair that had moved the more sensitive members of the team to tears. But the philosophers maintained that further empirical investigation was needed to determine for sure if the alien was conscious. All that the alien had done so far could have been done by a properly programmed machine, it was argued.

The suggestion was made that before the scientists simply accepted the alien at face value they should try a thought experiment: they should try to imagine what it would like if their minds worked along the same principles as were being suggested for the alien. It was argued by the more enthusiastic philosophers that this was a good way to test any theory of mind. The contention was that the thought experiment would reveal to the team the experiential character of having a neurophysiology like the alien's. Some of the team were dubious about this — it didn't look much like empirical enquiry — but they decided to give it a try in the interest of academic unity. It quickly emerged that the task was beyond them, not one of the team could even put himself in the position of running a simple computer program like Schank's, much less try to cope with the myriad complications of the alien's brain. Besides they didn't see how it could help. When they tried to imagine what it would be like to go through the same brain processes as another human (or even their own brain processes) they discerned that when understanding or consciousness did appear it did so like the final move in a magician's act — seemingly out of nowhere.

They gave up. The whole exercise had begun to seem futile. There were no empirical tests they could carry out to settle the issue and introspection was deemed unreliable. It was anathema to them to refuse to admit aliens as conscious no matter what the empirical/behavioural evidence before them. Then it occurred to them that something had to be wrong with their account of consciousness. The tempting suggestion that consciousness was not explainable except in terms of the causal power of human brain stuff should be resisted. They saw now that the same sort problems would arise in trying to decide if the consciousness of another human was ever called into question. The apparent criterion for deciding about consciousness was utterly unhelpful it could not be applied in any case.

The alien breathed a sigh of relief and departed leaving his tragic poetry to his biographers.

The problem with Searle's talk about causal powers is that it doesn't get us any further along the road to a solution. The causal power of anything is simply the power it has to cause something. We establish what causal powers a thing has been seeing what it causes. If I wanted to know if my computer has the power to cause a teleprinter to work I know what sorts of tests to apply (because I know what the criteria for teleprinter's working are) but things are much more difficult if I want to know if my computer has the power to cause mentation, at least they are if I am denied any independent way to establish that mentation is going on.

Searle's objections to accepting the answers and behaviour of computers or aliens as proof (or, it should be noted, disproof) of mentation leave us without any way of objectively determining when mentation is going on. Of course, if it weren't for Searle's objections we wouldn't be checking for the presence of 'causal powers' in the first place. The comparison of causal powers was supposed to show us when mentation was going on but we cannot compare the relevant causal powers unless we already have an independent test for mentation. Thus Searle's positive book is circular. Far from being a matter for empirical investigation the ascription of mentation seems to have become a matter for philosophical stipulation or alternatively an area of mystery.

Indeed a good deal of mystery surrounds Searle's positive book. He does not spell out what he means by causal powers nor does he indicate how we should go about deciding what the causal powers of a substance are. In the light of the comments I have made here it seems most unlikely that Searle has carried out empirical tests on his short list of proscribed materials for supporting mentation. In fact it is to be doubted whether Searle (or anyone else for that matter) even knows what such tests would look alike. It would be a considerable advance to even be told what the tests are testing for.

4.4.2.1 Summary

Right at the start of his paper Searle proposed a test for any theory of mind. How does his own theory of mind measure up to the test he set for all such theories? Is it possible to imagine what sort of diffference it might make to the character of our experience if our brains were made out of silicon instead of carbon? I have no more idea how Searle's theory of mind fares under his test that I did earlier with the strong AI account, which I suspect says more about his test than his theory of mind.

Whatever merit there might be in Searle's criticism of AI there is nothing to recommend his positive book. Of course Searle is right when he says that only substances which have the same (relevant) causal powers as the human brain can give rise to mentation. But this amounts to saying that only those substances which can cause mentation can cause mentation. So if Searle is right, he is so only at the expense of being uniformative.

4.4.3 The syntax/semantics distinction

We have seen that Searle is not convinced by strong AI's claim that all that is needed to give rise to mentation is the right formal computer program. He suggests that computers also need to be made from the right sort of stuff if they are ever to mentate. Searle completes his account of what present-day computers lack by saying that they have no semantics.

The syntax/semantics distinction is present in Searle's argument right from the introduction of the Chinese room example onwards:

> Well then, what is it that I have in the case of the English sentences
> that I do not have in the case of the Chinese sentences? The obvious
> answer is that I know what the former mean. [54]

Searle prefers to put off saying what this consists in and why we couldn't give it to a computer until later in his paper. The answer comes when he is trying to state some of the philosophical points which are implicit in his article:

'. . . could something think, understand and so on solely in virtue of being a computer with the right sort of program? Could instantiating a program, the right program of course, by itself be a sufficient condition of understanding?'

This I think is the right question to ask . . . and the answer to it is no.

'Why not?'

Because the formal symbol manipulations don't by themselves have any intentionality; they are quite meaningless; they aren't even symbol manipulations, since the symbols don't symbolize anything. In the linguistic jargon they have a syntax but no semantics. [55]

Searle goes on to add a little flesh to this:

The computer to repeat has a syntax but no semantics. Thus if you type into the computer '2 plus 2 equals?' it will type out '4'. but it has no idea that '4' means 4 or that it means anything at all. [56]

Presumably, the reason that we can't give a semantics to computers is to do with the materials out of which we build our machines. If a hunk of junk can't mentate, or have 'intentional states' as Searle would put it, then it can't have a semantics either. It is not made clear by Searle whether computers can't have a semantics because that would involve their having mental states — mentating — or because of some other special feature which a semantics has.

As with most of his other themes Searle repeats his contention that computers have syntax but not a semantics at every available opportunity. It can be found in his work right up to the present. But Searle never seems to develop any of his comments beyond their first statement. His case is repeated almost verbatim from publication to publication and seldom does it ever advance on the original.

4.4.3.1   What does a 'semantics' do?

But there are all sorts of questions that need answering about the syntax/ semantics distinction, not least of which is, 'What is a semantics?'. I grant that it would have been asking a bit much of Searle to have answered this question in his original article but he might well have clarified matters since. It is irritating to be told that there is something which humans have which computers cannot have and which is responsible (at least partially so) for the former's remarkable ability to understand stories or anything else and then not to be told what this something is.

Perhaps we can discover what a semantics is by finding out what it does. So what does a semantics do? We have already seen how Searle suggests that a semantics enables us to understand things but that is not so much an explanation as a restatement. Perhaps if we thought about what it would be like to not have a semantics we might be able to shed light on its function. It is clear from what Searle has to say about computers that without a semantics we might still be able to speak intelligently — where by speaking 'intelligently I mean nothing more than speaking in the same way as intelligent creatures, i.e. normal humans, speak.

It is therefore clearly a logical possibility that I should be in the middle of a conversation one day when suddenly I might 'lose' my semantics but that no-one would notice because I would just go on speaking apparently as normal. So, in order to speak intelligently I only need what computers have — a syntax and some syntactical rules for determining appropriate responses.

'Of course,' Searle might respond, 'that's all you would need, but you know — from personal experience — that you have much more than that. You understand stories in English but you can't understand Chinese stories; you have semantics for English and not for Chinese. Feigning amnesia isn't an answer here.'

My reply to this would be that it is true that I do know how to respond to stories in English and in 'knowing' what responses to make I am not consciously resorting to syntactical rules in the way a computer does, but nonetheless the possibility remains that I am in fact just using syntactical rules and that the use of these leads to understanding or gives rise to semantics if you prefer. It is no use reminding me that I don't understand (have a semantics for) Chinese stories although I can, with difficulty, apply syntactical rules to Chinese symbols and give back other Chinese symbols. The Chinese room example can work against Searle in this case; it just reminds us that unless a syntax (and its associated rules) are sublimated a semantics will not result. As we saw earlier, Searle's version of the Chinese room does not take account of the way computers (and perhaps humans) operate their syntax and syntactical rules. Perhaps getting a semantics from a syntax depends on not concentrating on operating the syntax. This phenomenon is not unique by any means, there are all sorts of tasks which we could not accomplish properly if we paid attention to their mechanics, these extend from running up a flight of stairs to speaking a foreign language.

Not only do we not have any conscious awareness of 'doing' anything when we understand the meaning of words but we don't even have a viable theory of why it should be that we have a semantics. So it seems that there is little or nothing except the character of our experience to suggest that semantics is not the result of the correct application of syntactical rules and as we have seen already, experience is anything but a reliable guide to the mechanics of mentation.

4.4.3.2 Does Smith know what 'long' means? The 'other minds' reply revisited

There are well established ways of determining if a person knows the meaning — has a semantics for — a given word. If we wanted to find out if Smith knew the meaning of the word 'long' we might ask Smith to define 'long'. It could be that he might respond with a definition: 'Of a set length or duration or of a great length or duration', and this would count as evidence for his understanding. Of course being able to give a definition is not critical;

Smith might not be able to define the word at all — this would be a little unusual in the present case, but what if the word were 'love' — and of itself that wouldn't be enough to show for certain that he didn't know what the word meant. We would be wise to pay attention to how, if at all, Smith uses, 'long', we should be interested if he were to maintain that 'long' is a long word. More likely would be subtle misunderstandings like only using 'long' in one sense rather than applying it in all its senses.

The point is that all the tests we might set Smith concern getting him to display an ability to apply the word correctly. But these sort of tests cut no ice with Searle for a computer might pass them as well as any human. So the price of denying that computers which can pass all the relevant Turing tests actually understand a natural language is that we should have no way of establishing for sure if anyone does. This extends to the first person case as well; think of how one goes about discovering if one 'really' understands a word like 'lithograph'. This was partly the point of the other minds reply to Searle. One has a choice between saying that behaviour of a certain (very great) cohesion and complexity is irrefutable evidence of mentation or one gives up on behaviour as evidence at all. The 'other minds' reply is roughly the view that the price of Searlean rigour is too high.

4.4.3.3   Who needs a semantics?
If Searle is right then there is nothing that we can 'do' with a semantics than we cannot do just as well without one. Our conversations would go along just as well as before. Research would proceed just as it ever did, composers would compose, we can even imagine philosophers having interesting discussions about how it should come about that we have a semantics. They would explain to others how discussions like theirs wouldn't be possible if people only had syntax — like machines. Appeals would still be made to the character of experience and the same people would agree or disagree as do now. To all intents and purposes everything would remain as it is at present — except no-one would really be discussing anything any more. All the world would contain would be the formal output of machines; apparent conversations would not so much be hot air as exhaust emissions, Isn't it lucky we have a semantics!

4.4.3.4   Conclusion
The evidence for the existence of a semantics is the nature of our experience and it is no part of my case to seriously deny that we understand language. However, we do not know how we come to understand and it is a possibility that semantics is simply syntax viewed from a different perspective. Even taking Searle's view, semantics is grounded in processes which do not have 'content': do neurotransmitters have content? No reason has been given against syntax as an explanation of the occurrence of semantics except that syntax has no content while semantics has and that argument will apply against every attempt to analyse semantics. Perhaps Searle doesn't want to carry out such an analysis but I am reluctant to ascribe such a view to him.

Searle's position leaves him with very few ways of ascertaining if anyone understands a natural language, if indeed he has any. He cannot rely on behavioural evidence since a computer might behave just as convincingly as a human. He has ruled out checking for the presence of brain states since a non-intentional computer could be designed to mimic those states. Nor would it be any use looking to see if the behaviour of the system in question is explainable in terms of its following a formal computer program, because we are all, according to Searle, the instantiations of any number of computer programs and while our behaviour could be explained fully in terms of following these programs that is not the explanation which Searle wants to take. It is even difficult to check to see if the thing in question is made from the right stuff because Searle doesn't make it clear what precisely we are looking for: no two individuals are made from exactly the same amount of atoms at each type. Until Searle (or someone else) comes up with an argument to the contrary, it remains a possibility that only certain combinations of atoms lead to mentation, all the rest simply give rise to the sort of uninteresting behaviour that computers are capable of. Of course I know that the critical combination occurs in David Anderson. What I would like to have is a position which enables Searle or anyone else to be as sure that I am mentating as I am myself. Searle's position is about as far removed from that happy condition as it is possible to be.

4.4.4   When is a simulation not just a simulation?

In summing up, Searle expresses himself surprised that anyone should ever have thought that a program which simulates understanding might also understand. After all, he reminds us, no-one supposes that a computer simulation of a five alarm fire will burn the neighbourhood down or that a simulated earthquake will lead to real casualties, so why should we expect understanding from a mere simulation of understanding.

The first thing to say here is that, at first glance, Searle's view, as always, appears to be quite in line with our intuitions. During election times we have all seen computer simulations of the effects of voters casting their vote in the way respondents to opinion polls have indicated. The commentator will type in a few variables: the projected number of voters, the percentage of the total vote that was polled for each of the parties at the last election, the results of the various polls and so on. In a moment we are shown a computer-generated pie chart showing the parliamentary cake divided between the contending parties. This projection might well turn out to be exactly right but no-one supposes that the computer running the simulation has any voting actually going on inside it. No-one is inclined to argue that since it is simulating human decision-making behaviour the computer is actually making decisions. The case with understanding appears to be just the same: of course the computer can simulate understanding but that is no reason to suppose the computer actually understands anything.

We might imagine a computer simulation of the chemical process of lactation. The machine would have elaborate programming which enabled it to tell us what grade and quantity of milk would be produced if grass of such and such a type were fed to a cow with the characteristics programmed into the computer. We could test the accuracy of the computer's simulation and might discover that it was always exactly right, but no-one would expect to get milk from it. Why then should anyone expect to get understanding from a computer just because it is accurately simulating understanding?

This sort of reasoning again demonstrates some of the dangers inherent in following intuition when trying to decide philosophical issues. Thinking about computer simulations of voting behaviour or lactation is apt to make us overlook some of the most important things about the proposed simulation of understanding. Indeed it is inclined to make us overlook the very features that are the most convincing about simulated understanding.

In order to bring this out I should first like to question the extent to which our initial thoughts about simulations accurately capture our expectations in the projected case of simulated understanding. Bear in mind that Searle originally proposed no ordinary simulation. What was on offer was a simulation that could not be discerned from the real thing on the basis of any of its associated phenomena. There was to be nothing human could do or say to demonstrate mentation that the computer could not do as well or say as convincingly. The computer was to appear to all of those who observed it exactly as a human. It was not just that we might systematically overlook some difference in behaviour between computer behaviour and human behaviour or that our tests might not be up to detecting any differences. The behaviour was to be perfect. From the outside, the simulation and the real thing were to be indistinguishable in principle.

Now suppose that we had a simulation of a five alarm fire that could not be distinguished by any difference in associated phenomena. What would we expect from *this* simulation? Flames, smoke, people being burned, property being lost, fire engines rushing about, these would all have to be present or we might be able to distinguish the simulation from the real thing. Under these circumstances it seems a little absurd to insist on a distinction between real and simulated fires (of course the general distinction is not in peril just its application to this sort of case). What we appear to have is two fires which would only be distinguishable by reference to their origins.

It seems that Searle is in a bind: he has conceded to much in setting up the example but he cannot settle for any less if he wants to make his point. If he allows a single behavioural difference to exist between computer performance and that of a normal human in similar circumstances then he has provided a wedge for AI researchers to drive into the Chinese room. On the other hand, by allowing phenomenal indistinguishability between a simulated mentation and 'real' thing Searle has heightened the attractiveness of strong AI because it now appears to be more in line with our intuitions and hence more plausible than might have originally seemed to be the case.

Take the following example. Imagine you woke up one morning to find yourself in hospital. When you had recovered your sense a little some (rather proud) doctors tell you that on your way home from work the evening before you were involved in a car accident which resulted in your hand being lost. However, thanks to the new technique of simul-surgery a perfect copy of your hand has been put in place of the old one. The hand is a perfect copy, if you pinch it pain will result and if you cut it will bleed. Your fingerprints are the same, in fact it is an atom for atom copy of the hand you had yesterday.

Now there is no doubt that the hand you now have is numerically different from the original but it would be straining credulity a little to say that it was an 'artificial' hand or that it was 'false'. Surely the entirely natural thing to say is that if you have a real hand that has all the features of your old hand except that instead of having grown their naturally it was placed on your wrist by surgeons. There is no inclination to say that you only have a 'simulated' hand even though it is a (perfect) simulation of your original hand.

Or imagine the case of someone offering you ten million simulated pounds. The notes in question are not forgeries but share all the features of real pounds. They are acceptable in any shop you please, bank managers will happily beat a path to your door to persuade you to deposit the simulated pounds in their branch and so on. Now does anyone feel inclined to refuse the offer of these notes? Would anyone seriously maintain that the pounds were in some sense less valuable than other pounds printed in the normal way? Would you refuse the offer?

What if someone prepared you a simulated meal. Choose whatever dishes you most desire and they are yours. The taste of the simulated food is exactly the same as any real food of the same type. The smell and texture are just the same as normal food and the simulated food will nourish you as well as the real variety. What point would there be in such circumstances in saying that the food was artificial or false or that real food was better? Would you really care which you ate?

Finally consider how you would react if someone offered you a simulated Rolls-Royce (or whatever your favourite car happens to be). The simulation would be as long and as sleek, as shiny and fast as the real thing. The simulated engine would run as well as a real engine and the simulated car would use as much petrol and attract as much road tax as any real Rolls. In what sense is the simulation less desirable than the real Rolls. Isn't much more sensible (in line with our intuitions) to simply say that there is no useful distinction to be drawn between the cars (or the hands, notes or meals).

Another feature of Searle's discussion of simulations which is worth drawing attention to is that in the cases of fires, floods, earthquakes and photosynbook the end product is describable in purely physical terms. This might be taken as an indication that Searle thinks of mentation as also describable in purely physical terms. This interpretation is given support by Searle's insistence that empirical tests can be applied to discover if a particular creature is mentating or just simulating mentation. However, there is a difficulty in ascribing this opinion to Searle: such a view would be counter-intuitive; after all the character of our experience is nmot such as to make us think of mentation in physical terms alone. This would be especially damaging to Searle since so much of his opposition to strong AI is built on the insights afforded to us by intuition. If Searle does think of understanding as a physical thing his claim to be accurately representing our intuitions is thereby greatly diminished and his whole case is weakened as a result.

4.4.4.1 Walter's response

There is a second sort of answer one can give to Searle. In his contribution to the Open Peer Commentary which accompanied Searle's article Donald Walter took the following line:

> Searle: No-one supposes that computer simulations of a five alarm fire will burn the neighbourhood down . . . . Why on earth should anyone suppose that a computer simulation of understanding actually understood anything?

> Walter: No-one supposes that a novelist's description of a five alarm fire will burn the neighbourhood down; why should anyone suppose that a novelist writing about understanding actually understood anything about it ? [57]

I take Walter's point but I am not entirely convinced that it is strictly relevant (perhaps Searle agrees with me because he did not reply to Walter's comments). The sort of simulations that Walter seems to have in mind are the sort that write up on a VDU that so many people would be killed and injured if such and such conditions were to hold during a five alarm fire. Indeed this seems to be the sort of simulation Searle often sounds as if he is talking about too:

> Let's program our favourite POP-10 with the formal program that simulates thirst. We can even program it to print out at the end 'Boy I am thirsty!' or 'Won't someone please give me a drink?', etc. Now would anyone suppose that we thereby have even the slightest reason to suppose that the computer is literally thirsty? Or that any simulation of other mental phenomena, such as understanding stories, feeling depressed or worrying about itemized reductions, must therefore produce the real thing? [58]

But of course the sort of program that prints up casualty figures or statements of thirst are better describable as computer predictions or models rather than simulations. As we have already seen, this wasn't the sort of program that Searle was talking about in his original article at all and it isn't the sort of program that anyone is seriously suggesting we ascribe mentation to.

4.4.4.2 Conclusion

Two sorts of reply are suggested to Searle. On the one hand we can point to computer simulations of five alarm fires as well as understanding and say that they are not to be contrasted with the real thing but with the equivalent of an author's description of the real thing. This sorty of reply agrees with Searle that simulations of understanding might not themselves do any understanding but explains this by saying that they aren't in that line of business in any case.

A second more radical approach is to say that some simulations go beyond merely copying the phenomenon simulated. Some simulations are like 'clones' of the real thing. I have suggested a number of examples where it seems to be appropriate to draw no distinction (except of origin) between real things and exceptionally good simulations of them. If a simulation of understanding is indistinguishable from the real thing then I maintain that it is not wrong to think of it as actually understanding. Does the following capture your intuitions or suggest that something is wrong with Searle's view?

> If more and more of the cells in your brain were to be replaced by integrated circuit chips, programmed in such a way as to keep the input–output function of each unit identical to that of the unit being replaced, you would in all likelihood just keep right on speaking as you are doing now except that you would eventually stop meaning anything by it. What we outside observers might take to be words would become for you just certain noises that circuits caused you make. [59]

4.4.5   Introduction

Searle makes two charges right at the end of *Minds, brains and programs* which have received very little attention. First he accuses strong AI of residual operationalism;

> I believe that if AI workers totally repudiated behaviourism and operationalism much of the confusion between duplication and simulation would be eliminated. [60]

Over the last two sections I hope to have showed that workers in AI are not confused between simulations and duplications, and consequently that they do not need to take the action Searle suggests. In fact I think it is Searle who has mis-read the situation and has failed to grasp how powerful a 'simulation' he has specified.

In this subsection I will deal with Searle's second and decisive charge that strong AI relies on a form of residual dualism. I will argue that Searle is right but that the consequences of this while fatal for strong AI are insignificant both for AI research and for the philosophical viewpoint which Searle has been trying to represent to us.

4.4.5.1   *To what extent are programs independent of the machines running them?*

As a lead-in to his accusation of dualism Searle makes the following point:

> ... strong AI only makes sense given the dualistic assumption that, where the mind is concerned, the brain doesn't matter. In strong AI (and in functionalism, as well) what matter are programs and

programs are independent of their realization in machines; indeed, as far as AI is concerned the same program could be realized by an electronic machine, a Cartesian mental substance or a Hegelian world spirit. [6]

This is the philosophical point which underlies the hunk of junk objection and the time has come to deal with it directly. In answer to the question, 'Are programs independent of their host machines?' the answer must be an unsatisfactory 'yes and no'. It all depends on what you mean by 'program'.

In order to make this clear let's take a very simple microcomputer example. The BBC micro has the facility to repeat a set of instructions until a condition is met. Thus it might print words from this sentence until it reached the end. A program for this might look something like the following:

```
10   REPEAT
20   READ word
30   PRINT word
40   UNTIL word="end"
```

Thus the machine would continue to read a new word from tis database and print it on its VDU until the word just printed was 'end', which happens to be the last word in the sentence we want to print up.

However, some other computers do not have REPEAT...UNTIL as an instruction so if they wanted to run the same program they would have to do something like this;

```
10   FOR loop=1 to 13
20   READ word
30   PRINT word
40   NEXT loop
```

What this program does is to read and print thirteen successive words (i.e. the number of words in the 'target' sentence) and thus the effect of running this program would be exactly the same as using the REPEAT...UNTIL version. There is a sense in which we are running the same program in each of these cases and the program would continue to be the same if we were to rig up a system involving some scales on one side of which were thirteen sheets of toilet paper and onto the other side of which dropped one sheet of toilet paper at a time until the scales balanced. Our apparatus could be set up in such a way as to drop a sheet of toilet paper each time a stone with a word from the target sentence written on it fell into the machine's display area. The whole process would end when the sentence was displayed. On the other hand, I am sure that the author of the BBC version would have a hard time trying to sue the authors of the author programs for infringement of copyright.

The question here is, do we have three programs with the same effect or one program in three different realizations? Searle is pretty clearly persuaded by the second option. I am not certain what to say. There might be a case for saying that if there isn't only one program here then at least the three programs are functionally equivalent. Even taking this view, it seems to me that there is a plausible case for distinguishing between the toilet paper program and the other two since not only are the observable effects quite distinguishable but the techniques used in the program are quite different from the microcomputer versions. I would be prepared to accept either of these differences but I am reluctant to take on both.

Now this may seem to put me in something of a bind. After all by being prepared to accept that a program is the same through different realizations which will presumably have different behavioural characteristics (suppose we had attached a printer to the micro instead of a VDU) have I not compromised the things I said earlier about a program giving rise to understanding when it produced behaviour of one sort and not when it produced different behaviour? Am I not committed to saying that the very same program both does and does not give rise to mentation?

I don't think I have said anything inconsistent and my reasons for insisting on this will be made clear by the end of the section. But before I spell them out I would like to look at Searle's main charge.

4.4.5.2   Is strong AI dependent on a form of residual dualism?
Searle sums up his case for a dualistic commitement in strong AI as follows:

> ... unless you accept some form of dualism, the strong AI project hasn't got a chance.
> ... Unless you believe that the mind is separable from the brain both conceptually and empirically — dualism in a strong form — you cannot hope to reproduce the mental by writing and running programs since programs must be independent of brains or any other particular forms of instantiation. If mental operations consist in computational operations on formal symbols, then it follows that they have no interesting connection with the brain ...
> This form of dualism ... is Cartesian in the sense that it insists that what is specifically mental about the mind has no intrinsic connection with the actual properties of the brain. This underlying dualism is masked from us by the fact that AI literature contains frequent fulminations against 'dualism'; what the authors seem to be unaware of is that their position presupposes a strong version of dualism. [62]

Searle's main point takes us right back to his definition of strong AI which you will recall was that 'minds are certain sorts of (admittedly very sophisticated) programs' — minds can't be programs because programs are independent of their realization and that involves us in the familiar problems of mind–body dualism. Searle is absolutely right. Strong AI does have a dualist commitment and is, as a direct result, untenable. But this complete victory for Searle is not the end of the story by any means.

4.4.5.3   The systems reply–strong AI gets tough!

Right at the start of my consideration of Searle I was critical of the strong AI – weak AI distinction, the time has now come to complete that criticism.

In my view Searle has never taken the systems reply with anything like the seriousness it deserves but, that said, its advocates seem to have been reluctant to really press it for the systems reply (which is little more that AI orthodoxy) is inconsistent with strong AI! The whole point of making the systems reply is to emphasize that minds are not programs. The statement that minds are programs is a straightforward category mistake. The systems reply insists that systems mentate. This stands in direct opposition to the claim that minds are programs — once again, it is not programs that mentate, mentation is a characteristic of certain systems of which we are the only absolutely clear example. The reason that the inconsistency has not before been picked up is, I think, to do with the second half of Searle's definition of strong AI which says that 'computers, properly programmed, may be said to have minds. which is an affirmation of the central claim of the systems reply. This second half of Searle's origianl definition stands alone as a definition of what I will call 'tough AI' and when tough AI is conjoined with the claim that 'minds are certain sorts of program' the result is an inconsistency. It is this inconsistency which dogs Searle's work and which is the main cause of its undoing.

To return to Searle's accusation of dualism and to complete my defence against the charge of inconsistency which I raised against myself above I should like to note in the first place that I have never held that programs are independent of their realizations in the way Searle thinks advocates of strong AI must do. Consistent with tough AI, it seems entirely obvious to me that the effect of a program (what it does) will be influenced greatly by the nature of the hardware which it is controlling — printers just don't have the same effect as VDUs.

It does not bother me to say that if a program P is run on machine A the result is mentation whereas if P is run on B the result might not be mentation. This does not have anything to do with the 'actual properties' (whatever that might mean) of A and B but points out that system PA may have different characteristics from system PB.

For example, we do not look for different 'actual properties' in the brain of someone born blind to explain the possibility that he doesn't understand the word 'red' fully — that he can't use the word in all appropriate contexts. The explanation for this 'failure of intentionality' is to be found in what computer enthusiasts might describe as defective peripherals (his eyes don't work) not in the 'actual properties' of the man's brain or in the computer program that he is instantiating.

I continue to maintain that a computer running a program which takes account of the robot reply might well literally understand words like 'tree', 'red', 'dog', etc., but if the very same program were to be run in a machine whose peripherals (eyes, ears, touch pads and so on) were all defective might not only result in a failure to actually understand such words but might even completely fail to result in any mentation. I don't think this is inconsistent, on the contrary it is not only consistent, it is also perfectly obvious.

4.4.5.4 *Conclusion*

Searle has shown half of what he set out to show. He has failed to demonstrate that programs are independent of the machines on which they run in any important sense. There are good reasons for accepting two things: first, the very same program will not run on different machines, though, it will possibly have a functional equivalent which will run; secondly, what a system may be properly thought of doing as doing is not solely dependent on the program or on the 'actual properties of the hardware, but is a function of the union of these two things.

I accept that Searle has shown that strong AI does rely on a form of residual dualism. However, this is not very significant since strong AI is not a consistent view in any event. The position I think best represents the views of actual workers in AI is tough AI and this is both consistent and free from any residual dualism. Tough AI embodies the systems approach and is untouched by any of Searle's criticisms which, for the most part, do not take the systems approach seriously anyway.

5

A classical problem

5.1 INTRODUCTION

Whatever its other merits classical logic cannot lay claim to being a formalization of the normal human reasoning process. In the course of the next section I am going to consider in some depth one particular way in which classical logic fails to mirror the human deductive process: I will be considering contradictions — how we handle them, how classical logic deals with them and how some logicians have suggested that classical logic should be changed in order to handle them.

Consider the following rather trivial example. Det. Smith of the Yard is studying a dossier on a robbery suspect and is considering whether to call the person in for an interview. The dossier has been compiled by two of Smith's inexperienced junior offices, PC Jones and PC Brown. According to Jones, the suspect is male and around 6 ft tall; according to Brown the suspect is male and around 5 ft 2 in in height. Suppose that the robbery was known to have been committed by 'a tall man', what would Det Smith's likely reaction be? He would doubtless call the constables in and sort out an accurate picture of the suspect. If Smith had been limited to treating the information in the dossier like premises for an argument in a piece of classical reasoning, then he would have been in serious trouble because he would have contradictory premises and could have quite properly inferred anything he liked. As it was he did not just infer anything but was able to resolve the contradiction. This is a case of a human handling a 'noticed' contradiction, but what if Smith hadn't noticed the contradiction — what if he had just continued to consider the question of whether the suspect should be brought into the station? Although Smith could draw any conclusion at all (for example, 'Paris is the capital of the United States of America') without committing any logical error there are only certain sorts of conclusion which Smith would in fact draw: the suspect is/is not worth bringing in, etc.

The problem before us is this: can we develop a logic which could be implemented on a computer to help it to continue to reason in situations where contradictions might have been 'fed into' it as premises, but have not been noticed?

The aim of this section will be to answer this question in the affirmative and to formulate and present a logic which might be implemented on a computer in order to help it not just to cope with contradictions but to retain the classical 'look' which much of the human deductive process has.

While superficially quite like some other logics which are already well known in the logical community this one has a semantics which makes it unique, and it is also specially resistant to the philosophical objections which may be levelled at its close relatives.

The logic which I will present had its origins in an undergraduate dissertation on Graham Priest's LP system, but in its first version it suffered from one of the major ills of LP — its semantics could not, in the final analysis, be made coherent. This difficulty led to a re-examination of the system's semantics which in the present version have been replaced with semantics which both have better application to the computer's needs and can be made coherent.

This section will include a discussion of the LP system which is representative of the sort of approach to contradictions which I call the 'logics for paradoxes' approach. I will also discuss Lewis's ideas about what humans do when they cope with contradictions.

5.2   LIVING WITH PARADOXES

Quine sums up the early attempts to deal with the contradictions in mathematics and set theory thus:

> Consider . . . the crisis which was precipitated in the foundations of mathematics, at the turn of the century, by the discovery of Russell's paradox and other antinomies of set theory. These contradictions had to be obviated by ad hoc devices; our mathematical myth — making became deliberate and evident to all. [1]

It is in very much the same spirit of dissatisfaction with attempts to avoid rather than to solve the problems that paradoxes pose that Graham Priest writes in his article 'The logic of paradox'. He is one of an apparently growing group of logicians whose reaction to paradoxes is to try to incorporate them into their logic. This requires a resolution of the difficulties that result from accepting what are, after all, contradictions.

5.2.1   What's wrong with contradictions?
In any system of logic where

$$A \ \& \ -A \ \text{entails} \ B$$

(where B is any arbitrary formula) holds (for example, classical logic) the acceptance of a contradition results in the loss of deductive selectivity, that is, all the formulae of such a system become provable as theorems!

5.2.2   Logics for paradoxes
If we are to live with paradoxes it seems that the price we must pay is a serious revision of our logic. Those logicians who, like Priest, have taken up

this challenge have thereby set themselves the task of creating logics for paradoxes. Given the widely accepted failure of the philosophical community to arrive at an appealing non ad hoc answer within the parameters of classical logic, this latest approach was perhaps inevitable. For all that, it does not yet represent mainstream thinking or a route which particularly appeals to me. However, the current preoccupation in the literature with 'alternative' logics suggests that this trend cannot and should not be ignored.

There are quite a few logics for paradoxes around but I will confine myself to discussing Priest's because his is one of the clearest and most businesslike, and it makes important advances on the work done in this field already by Kleene (1952), [2] Lukasiewicz (1920) [3] and Asenjo (1966) [4]. Thus an examination of Priest is an examination of some of the very best work that is being done in this area.

My concern in what follows will not be to defend philosophers like Tarski and Von Neumann from the charge, which Priest makes, that their respective attempts to deal with paradoxes are ad hoc defences of classical reasoning. I will be concentrating on Priest's attempt to develop a paradox-tolerant system of logic — that is to say, a system of logic which contains at least one formula, f, which is not deducible from A & −A. I will find that there are a number of important reasons why we should reject LP, but the lessons which can be learned from Priest's failure will provide the basis of a logic for which there are far better prospects.

5.2.3 Correcting classical logic's mistake

According to Priest, classical logic is founded, at least in part on an error:

> Classical logic errrs in assuming that no sentence can be both true and false. We wish to correct this assumption. If a sentence is both true and false, let us call it 'paradoxical' (p). If it is true but not false we will call it 'true only' (t) and similarly for 'false only' (f). [5]

We are further told that . . . .

> A sentence is true iff its negation is false. hence the negation of a true and false sentence is false and true, i.e. paradoxical. The negation of a true only sentence is false only . . . the negation of a false only sentence is true only. [6]

On the basis of these assertions Priest presents us with the following tables for negation, conjunction and disjunction:

−		&	t	p	f		V	t	p	f		⇒	t	p	f
t	f		t	t	p	f		t	t	t	t		t	t	p	f
p	p		p	p	p	f		p	t	p	p		p	t	p	p
f	t		f	f	f	f		f	t	p	f		f	f	t	t

In order to clarify matters a little, Priest gives us some idea of the reasoning that leads to these tables:

If A is t and B is p, then both A and B are true. Hence A & B is true. However, since B is false, A & B is false. Thus A & B is paradoxical.

If A is f and B is p, then both A and B are false. Hence A & B is false. If A & B were true as well, then both A and B would be true, but A is false only. Hence A & B is f. [7]

Priest allows that the tables for disjunction and implication can be generated by the convention of defining A ∨ B and A ⇒ B in terms of '&'s and '−'s in the following way:

$$A \lor B =^{df} -(-A \ \& \ -B)$$
$$A \Rightarrow B =^{df} -(A \ \& \ -B)$$

In LP both t and p are designated values because 'both are the values of true sentences'. Priest spells this out as follows:

> Formally let L be a propositional language whose set of propositional variables of P. Let v:P→{t,p,f} (i.e., v is a valuation of the propositional variables). Let v$^+$ be the natural extension of v to all the sentences of L using the above truth tables. If E is a set of sentences of L, we define;
>
> E ⊢ A iff there is no v such that v$^+$ (A)=f, but for all B ∈ E, v$^+$ (B)=t or p.
>
> ⊢ A iff ∅ ⊢ A (i.e. for all v, v$^+$ (A)=t or p) [8]

On the subject of tautologies, Priest tells us that:

> A is a two valued tautology iff ⊢ A [9]

These innovations have the effect of making invalid a number of classically valid deductions. This was, of course, to be expected; indeed it was, in a sense, the point of the exercise. The minimum requirement of a paradox-tolerant logic is that A & −A ⊢ B should fail, but the scope of the failures in LP goes well beyond this. The following classically valid deductions do not hold in LP:

$$A \ \& \ -A \vdash B$$
$$A, -A \lor B \vdash B$$
$$A \Rightarrow (B \ \& \ -B) \vdash -A$$
$$A \Rightarrow B, B \Rightarrow C \vdash C$$
$$A, A \Rightarrow B \vdash B$$
$$A \Rightarrow B, -B \vdash -A$$

Even philosophers who do not take a special interest in formal logic will realize at a glance the serious injury to deductive power which this list represents. Priest himself admits that 'We cannot give these inferences up without crippling classical reasoning' [10]. He puts a brave face on though and proposes that we regard the listed inferences not as invalid (which in reality they are) but as 'quasi-valid'. 'Quasi' because they are truth-preserving provided there are no paradoxical sentences involved. We are urged to accept the following methodological maxim:

MM
Unless we have specific grounds for believing that paradoxical sentences are occurring in our argument, we can allow ourselves to use both valid and quasi-valid inferences. [11]

Now that we have seen what Priest has to say in support of LP, it is time to assess his arguments. I would like to draw attention to five major differences between LP and classical logic:

(1) LP has quite distinctive semantics.
(2) LP employs a novel account of entailment.
(3) LP has a narrower application for the term 'two-valued tautology' than classical logic.
(4) The set of LP valid inferences is a subset of the set of classically valid inferences (the simple consequence of (1) and (2) above).
(5) Users of LP are, for all practical purposes, obliged to adopt the methodological maxim, MM.

5.2.4   The semantics of LP

One of the most noticeable features of the LP truth tables (which define the meaning of LP's logical operators) is the degree of apparent overlap between them and their classical counterparts. Indeed, if all the sections of the former tables which result from one or more of the variables taking the value p were crossed out, what remains would be exactly the same in appearance as the standard classical tables which are familiar in systems like those of Lemmon and Copi.

Because of our familiarity with truth tables like these it is easy to forget that the t's and f's in a Copi table have a quite different meaning from the t's and f's in the LP tables. In classical logic (and in ordinary discourse) if we say that a proposition is 'true' we mean that it is not 'false'. Priest appears to be in agreement with this when he tells us that 'a sentence is true iff its negation is false' [12]. After all this does nothing more than capture our intuitions about truth and falsity under negation, but any claim which Priest might have had to intuitive appeal for his system vanishes when he introduces the notion of a proposition being 'true and false'. The temptation was to read Priest's views about negation in a classical way, i.e. 'a sentence is true (only) iff its negation is false (only)', and this seems hardly worth questioning.

If Priest's notion of 'truth' is such that 'true' propositions may also be 'false' then it seems that nothing can be taken for granted. How can we be certain that this sort of truth behaves in the same way under negation as classical truth? Priest's comments are stipulatory and while this is not unusual in logic it is here obscured both by both notions being called 'truth' and by the methodological maxim which makes it sound as if Priest's truth is an extension of classical truth. The change Priest is proposing is not mere extension, it is a whole-scale revision of the concept of truth. Indeed, the revision which Priest has in mind has the effect of completely altering what is meant by 'truth'. It is as if we woke up one morning and found that 'white' had been extended to include 'black'. Many of the uses which we used to have for 'white' would appear to be unaffected by the change but in reality we would have lost the conceptual difference between black and white. Priest has lost what was essential to the difference between truth and falsity by allowing them to be compatible. Once he has taken the step of permitting propositions to be both true and false his semantics needs to be justified, not just stipulated. It is difficult to imagine any means by which such a semantics could be given justification; just what would convince us that truth is compatible with falsity?

It might be thought that the existence of propositions such as, 'This sentence is false' and paradoxes like Russell's paradox show that some 'true' sentences are also 'false'. I do not agree. The existence of such sentences shows us that something is wrong to be sure but I would sooner abandon all self reference and set theory than take the course which Priest follows. The effect of going along with Priest is to abandon the notion of 'truth' and the cost of this is greater than the loss of set theory or even the whole of mathematics! I am not convinced that the time has come when we should abandon attempts to find a non ad hoc solution within classical logic to the problems that paradoxes pose. But should such a time ever come it would not be signal to take the drastic measures which Priest urges, though, as I have indicated, other serious steps would be in order.

These comments not withstanding I would like to turn to a consideration of the logic which Priest offers. It should be noted that in formulating a paradox-tolerant logic no committment is made to the actual existence of any paradoxical sentence, but only, at most, to the possibility of some such sentences.

5.2.5   LP's entailment relation

If there is one place where Priest is likely to err in developing LP, it is in his account of entailment. Not only Priest, but anyone who wants to produce a logic within the broad parameters in which he is working, will face the same difficulty.

Let's examine the problem. There are nine possible cases of entailment, each of which requires to be ruled allowable or not. The cases are determined by the truth values which are taken (overall) by the premises and the conclusion, and they are as follows:

	A entails	B
1.	t	t
2.	t	p
3.	t	f
4.	p	t
5.	p	p
6.	p	f
7.	f	t
8.	f	p
9.	f	f

Even inconsistent logics like LP should be truth-preserving — they should not allow as legitimate any argument which proceeds from true premises to a false conclusion — if they fail this test they fail altogether. The usual procedure is to 'designate' one or more values in the system. B is said to be a consequence of A (in some logic L) if, for all admissible valuations, B is assigned a designated value whenever A is:

> . . . designated values are thought of as being true or as degrees of truth, whereas undesignated values are ways of failing to be true, or degrees of falsity. [13]

Thus we might expect t to be a designated value and f to be undesignated in LP (just as their classical counterparts are). Our expectations would not be misplaced and this has the immediate consequence of ruling 'invalid' inferences like case 3 and ruling 'valid' inferences like cases 7, 8 and 9. The problem which Priest has is whether to designate p or to leave it undesignated. Priest's answer is both brief and unsatisfactory; p should be designated like t because 'both are the values of true sentences'. But by the same token Priest could have left p undesignated because p and f are both the values of false sentences! If we are to decide the issue we will need to have recourse to other arguments.

One solution might be to treat sentences taking the value p as if they took the value f when they appeared on the right-hand side of an entailment sign, and as t when they appeared on the left. In other words, if E is a set of sentences of L, we define:

> $E \vdash A$ iff there is no v such that $v+ (A)=f$
> or p
> but for all $B \in E$, $v+ (B)=t$ or p

This would have the advantage of being highly truth-preserving, but there is an equally high price to pay for this advantage. Given this reading of the entailment sign, even $A \vdash A$ is an invalid inference. Another solution might be to define entailment in the following way:

> $E \vdash A$ iff there is no v such that $v+ (A)=f$
> but for all $B \in E$, $v+ (B)=t$

but in this case the logic is not paraconsistent (for example, A & −A ⊢ B holds).

This leaves us with only one remaining alternative, which designates t and leaves f undesignated.

We might define entailment in the following way:

> E ⊢ A iff there is no v such that v+ (A)=f
> or p
> but for all B ∈ E, v+ (B)=t

but here again the resulting logic is not paraconsistent.

So it seems that we are left with Priest's reading of entailment but without a satisfactory phiosophical justification of our choice. It rather looks as if the choice we have made is ad hoc. The price we have to pay for Priest's entailment is also a stiff one — this time truth preservability is undermined. Arguments which proceed from premises taking t to conclusions taking p (case 2) or from premises taking p to conclusions taking p (case 5) may, if p is read as 'true and false', be reasonably thought of as proceeding from true premises to false conclusions. Yet in LP these are both valid forms of inference. This once more raises the question of what Priest means when he talks about truth or when he assigns a sentence the value p.

5.2.6 A restriction on the notion of a two-valued tautology

As I mentioned above, Priest wants to restrict the use of the term 'two-valued tautology'. I want to do little more than to note this innovation. What we are actually told is that:

> A is a two valued tautology iff ⊢ A [14]

Clearly the significance we attach to the appearance of p's in the main column of the truth table of A depends on whether p is a designated value or not (in the light of what we have just said about the entailment relation it seems unlikely that there would be any system of paradox-tolerant logic in which p was not a designated value).

5.2.7 LP's methodological maxim, MM

Obivously we expect some classically valid inferences to be invalid in any system of paradox-tolerant logic. Indeed, we have seen that in order to be a paradox-tolerant logic, a system must rule invalid A & −A ⊢ B at the very least. However, the number and nature of the classically valid deductions which do not hold in LP is, quite simply, too great to be tolerated. To his credit, Priest does not try to disguise the fact that he has created a system which is 'crippled' but sets out to make it workable.

The device which Priest uses to accomplish this is the adoption of MM. This raises the question of how far we are able to identify paradoxes; can we spot them all the time or might they sometimes escape our notice? Clearly much hangs on the answer to this. If, as seems likely, paradoxes are capable of going unnoticed (even on the rare occasions when we are actually looking for them) then we will have little option but to 'play safe' and always use LP without MM. After all, the acceptance of 'quasi-valid' deductions would, under the circumstances, be more than a little rash. On the other hand, if we are certain that paradoxes can (and will) always be uncovered then we can accept MM and then LP will be on firmer ground, although I, for one, would be a lot happier to adopt a maxim which encouraged us to check our premises at the outset. Experience shows that paradoxes are often very difficult to uncover and in the case of Cantor and Frege paradoxes escaped notice and were unwittingly adopted. In the case of Cantor's axiomatization of set theory, the problem is well highlighted because even after we have discovered that they lead to paradoxes we are not inclined to abandon any of his premises.

Whatever merits there may have been for adopting MM in the context in which Priest devised the system, the particular requirements of the AI context make it unsuitable. You will recall that the problem that we are trying to get an answer for is concerned primarily with ordinary contradictions. These are more plentiful than the samll specialized group of contradictions which concern Priest. Ordinary contradictions are much more common than paradoxes and we are especially concerned to find a way of handling unnoticed contradictions, to find a logic that will enable a computer to continue to reason even when it has contradictory premises. Since the benefits of MM can only be enjoyed if the computer notices the contradictory nature of its premises, it follows that MM has no role to play in the central the central case which poses a problem for computer reasoning.

It seems then that there are good reasons for trying to do without MM. But if we try to operate LP without MM we soon feel the loss. Quite apart from being exceptionally inconvenient, the loss of disjunctive syllogism, modus ponens and the rest is highly counter-intuitive. My original approach was to stipulate different truth tables in place of those urged by Priest. It turns out that there are a number of prima facie suitable tables for conjunction and negation which can be used to generate a grand total of 27 systems.

There are a number of reasons why this approach was and is unsatisfactory. In the first place it does not get around the major philosophical objections which I have raised against LP, although to be fair it was never designed to overcome these. The idea was to produce a more effective logic than Priest's while staying within the same boundaries as Priest sets himself, and in these terms my approach was successful. It will also become apparent when I come to develop a logic for the computer situation that we need a four-valued logic, not a three-valued logic like LP (actually there is some question as to whether Priest's logic is even a real three-valued logic or if it just reassigns the traditional two values).

In the light of these difficulties it is probably best to go back to the drawing board and start again. But before I present an outline of my logic I would like to spend some time looking at some other approaches to the problems to which inconsistency gives rise.

5.3 A SECOND APPROACH TO CONTRADICTIONS

Earlier I suggested that the way human beings handle contradictions is not the way suggested by classical logic, because even when we argue from inconsistent premisses we do not completely lose deductive selectivity — we do not just come up with any old conclusion — thus if Det. Smith simultaneously believes that Brown is 6 ft tall and 5ft 2 in tall there is no danger that he will argue from these premisses to 'Paris is the capital of the United States of America' or Anderson has two noses' or any other such nonsense.

There are at least two reasons why these conclusions are unacceptable. In the first place they are both known falsehoods (which partly explains their choice as examples) and we may assume that Det. Smith knows that Paris is not the capital of the United States of America and that Anderson does not have two noses. In human reasoning there is a demonstrable reluctance to accept a known falsehood as a conclusion to any argument, or to use a known falsehood as a premiss. Classical logic reflects the second of these concerns by noting that false conclusions properly follow from false premisses and takes account of the first concern by stipulating that an argument form must be truth-preserving before it may be regarded as valid and by allowing *reductio ad absurdum* as a way of calling premisses into question. Thus the notion of truth preservation is well catered for in traditional logic.

There is also a second reason why humans do not feel happy to draw just any old conclusion when arguing from inconsistent premisses or even when arguing from premisses which are both consistent and true. This second reservation may be illustrated by the following examples.

From 'Anderson's book is well written' and 'If and only if Anderson's book is well written then Anderson will be awarded a literary prize' it seems perfectly acceptable to conclude 'Anderson will be awarded a literary prize'. However, from the same premisses it would be normally thought unacceptable to conclude 'Either Mars supports life or Mars does not support life'. Despite our intuitions both are equally valid argument forms in classical logic; this stems from the fact that neither argument can have a false conclusion when its premisses are true.

From 'Anderson's book is well written' and 'It is not the case that Anderson's book is well written' and 'If and only if Anderson's book is well written then Anderson will be awarded a literary prize' it seems perfectly in order to accept either of the following conclusions: 'Anderson will be awarded a literary prize' or 'It is not the case that Anderson will be awarded a literary prize'. But it is unacceptable to conclude that 'Smith will be the first man to land on Venus' or 'Mrs Thatcher will lose the next election', yet each of these combinations of premisses and conclusion has a form which is classically valid.

The reason why we find the acceptable arguments above acceptable and reject the others is fairly obvious; in the acceptable arguments the premisses and conclusion are relevant to each other and in the other cases premisses and conclusion are quite irrelevant one to the other. Classical logic takes no account of relevance and it has been suggested that this is a major flaw which can only be corrected by supplementing or even replacing traditional logic with a relevance logic.

So it seems that in human argumentation there are two separate merits to be sought — truth preservation and relevance:

> But relevance has lately been praised not — or not only — as a separate merit, but rather as something needed to ensure preservation of truth. Classical implication does preserve truth, to be sure, so long as sentences divide neatly into the true and the false. But when the going gets tough and some sentences are true and false both (or neither), then the relevance logician gets going; then his relevant implication preserves truth and some classical implication doesn't. [15]

Lewis gives some evidence of the way in which failing to preserve relevance might lead to a failure to preserve truth. Suppose that A is both true and false, it follows that −A is both false and true and that A & −A, being the conjunction of two truths, is also true. Let B be false and not true. Under these conditions the classically valid implication *ex falso quodlibet*:

$$A \ \& \ −A \vdash B$$

fails to preserve truth since it proceeds from a true premiss to a false conclusion. Given the same conditions disjunctive syllogism will give rise to similar difficulties, for since A is true, A ∨ B is true, thus:

$$A \lor B, \ −A \vdash B$$

leads from two true premisses to a false conclusion.

So it appears that even if we have no other reason for wanting to include relevance in our account of implication the relevance logician has shown that we need to include it, for otherwise we jeopardize truth preservation.

Lewis looks at three versions of the claim that a sentence may be true only, false only, both true and false or — possibly — neither true nor false. this contention leads to the provision of either three- or four-valued semantics according to which a sentence is true if it is either true only or true and false and a sentence is false when it is either false only or true and false. We may summarize Lewis's coverage of the three versions as follows.

Version E (Dunn, Belnap and Mackinson) allows valuations to make sentences neither true nor false as well as both true and false and thus has a four-valued semantics:

> The implications so validated turn out to just those given by the first degree fragment of the well known Anderson–Belnap logic E of entailment. [16]

Disjunctive syllogism and *ex falso quodlibet* are not validated and neither are the following irelevant implications:

A ⊢ B ∨ –B
A & –A ⊢ B ∨ –B

Version RM (Dunn, Dunn and Mackinson) only allows valuations to make sentences true, or false or both and hence has only a three-valued semantics.

> The implications so validated are those given by the first degree fragment of the partly relevant logic R — mingle [17]

This version validates the irrelevant implication:

A & –A ⊢ B ∨ –B

but not

A ⊢ B ∨ –B

or disjunctive syllogism or *ex falsol quodlibet.*

Finally, Version LP (Priest), as we have seen, allows valuations to make sentences true, false, or both and thus has a three-valued semantics:

> The implications validated are those given by the first degree fragment of Priest's 'logic or paradox' LP [17]

this version validates both of the irrelevant implications:

A ⊢ B ∨ –B
A & –A ⊢ B ∨ –B

but not disjunctive syllogism or *ex falso quodlibet* and as we have seen above there are many more sorts of implication ruled out by version LP:

> All this may help illuminate the technicalities of relevant logic, but of course it is worthless as an intuitive vindication of relevance unless somehow it makes sense that sentences can be both true and false. [18]

Lewis notes that there are two accounts of how sentences can be both true and false currently being canvassed and he declares himself unpersuaded by either.

The first account is the radical answer of Priest and Routley which has it that we don't need explanation but only liberation from a dogma of traditional thinking; perhaps some sentences simply are true and false: we have noted some examples already above but to these may be added contradictions of our own making:

> The department can make it true or false by declaration that a dissertation is accepted. If by mistake or mischief both declarations were made, might both succeed? [19]

Further benefits might flow from this proposal in the fields of physics and theology, where thorny problems might be solved if we were allowed to entertain inconsistent solutions. Lewis has a simple and direct way of dealing with Routley and Priest which I fully endorse:

The reason we should reject this proposal is simple: nothing is, and nothing could be literally both true and false. This we know for certain and *a priori* and without any exception for especially perplexing subject matters. The radical case for relevance should be dismissed just because the hypobook it asks us to entertain is inconsistent.

That may seem dogmatic. And it is: I am affirming the very book that Routley and Priest have called into question and — contrary to the rules of debate — I decline to defend it. Further I concede that it is indefensible against their challenge, since they have called so much into question that I have nothing to push against. So much the worse for the demand that philosphers must always be ready to defend their theses under the rules of debate. [20]

I have already put forward much the same view when considering Priest directly so there is nothing much to add here, except to mention that my comments extend to Routley as well. However, one small detour might be in order. After all, there is a view made popular by Quine which maintains that all beliefs are ultimately revisable. To be sure, the law of non-contradiction would be one of the last of our beliefs to undergo revision, but it is revisable in principle.

I have no sympathy with this view. In the first place I can imagine no situation in which I would actually be prepared to revise the law of non-contradiction. And suppose I underwent a change of heart and asserted that, as a matter of fat, there are (say) some particles which have momentum but no position (and not just that we can only measure either a particle's momentum or its position but not both at once) or that light literally both travels in straight lines and in waves (and not just that there is equally good evidence for both views) , then what would I be saying? Unless the meanings of the terms involved have changed (which, *ex hypothesi,* they have not) I would not appear to be making sense. How could anything be both a perfectly straight line and a wave? If we accept that some contradictions are true then we give up the ability to coherently communicate the fact. If Quine and his followers are right then they might as well be wrong for all the difference it would make. It seems to me that given that they hold the view that there are true contradictions there is nothing Quineans can say to show that there is anything wrong with maintaining that there could not be any true contradictions. By allowing so much to be called into question, Quineans forfeit their ability tao take part in this, or any other, debate.

The second account of how sentences might be both true and false is more conservative and comes from Dunn and Routley (who puts forward both accounts) and Lewis thinks that he has, by reading between the lines, detected much the same account from Belnap. Here we abandon talk about actual (ontological) truth and falsity and concentrate instead on truth or falsity according to some body of information:

It might be someone's system of beliefs, the data bank of a question answering computer (Belnap's example), an almanac or encyclopaedia or textbook, a theory or a system of mythology or even a work of fiction. [21]

The aim is to achieve a concentration of truth according to a corpus which, when the corpus is mostly correct, will serve as a good (though not infallible) guide to truth simpliciter. Lewis lays down the following four conditions:

(1) A sentence is true if it is explicitly affirmed by the corpus.
(2) Truth is not limited to what is explicitly in the corpus but is, to some extent, closed under implication.
(3) An inconsistency in the corpus does not make everything true according to the corpus so truth according to the corpus is not closed under classical implication.
(4) A sentence is false according to the corpus iff its negation is true according to the corpus.

Such a proposal cannot be used to motivate a three-valued semantics because a corpus is more likely to be incomplete than inconsistent and so it is almost inevitable that some sentences will be neither true nor false according to the corpus, though it does look:

> as if it could give us an intuitive uniform motivation for the four valued semantics of Version E and for the resulting case against irrelevant implication. [22]

However, Lewis does not think that this proposal actually succeeds in giving us an intuitive vindication of relevance. He sees nothing wrong with saying that some sentences may be true and false according to some corpus of information, or with saying that we have a 'legitimate and useful' conception of truth that does satisfy the four conditions outlined, but as a matter of fact Lewis thinks that our conception does not work in a way that fits the four-valued semantics. Indeed, Lewis has quite a different idea in mind — he believes that we actually use a method of fragmentation to contain inconsistencies. he gives the following example of what he has in mind:

> I used to think that Nassau Street ran roughly east–west; and the nearby railroad ran north–south; and that the two were roughly parallel. (By 'roughly' I mean 'to within 20°'.) So each sentence in an inconsistent triple was true according to my beliefs but not everything was true according to my beliefs. My system of beliefs was broken into (overlapping) fragments. Different fragments came into operation in different situations, and the whole system of beliefs never manifested itself at once. [23]

So Lewis's view is that it is the fragmentation of our corpus of beliefs which prevents those inconsistent beliefs which we hold from doing more damage. Something about the way we store our beliefs or something to do with the way in which we use those beliefs for the most part keeps each fragment consistent. On those occasions when a fragment does contain an inconsistency we may either spot the inconsistency and do something about it or miss the inconsistency and thereby do further damage to the integrity of our corpus of beliefs:

> Insofar as we avoid trouble with the inconsistencies (and similar trouble with errors that do not make inconsistency) we do it by not freely mixing premises out of different fragments . . . In a nutshell, truth according to a fragmented corpus is not closed under conjunction, at least not under conjunction across fragments. Likewise falsehood according to a fragmented corpus is not closed under disjunction. [24]

This has the effect of undermining the relevance logician's case for relevance for now Lewis can argue that it has not been shown that failing to take account of relevance will lead to a failure to preserve truth. The argument runs as follows: a complete corpus may well contain a sentence A and its negation −A but there is no guarantee that these will occur together in any particular fragment, and since truth according to a corpus is not closed under conjunction across fragments, it is thus possible that A & −A might still not be true according to the corpus, thus giving the lie to the relevance logician's claims. Hence, according to Lewis we must look for another way in which sentences can be thought of as being both true and false if we are to provide a vindication of relevance.

Lewis's suggestion is that we look to ambiguity. The sentence 'Scrooge walked along the bank on this way to the bank' is obviously ambiguous. This sentence may be true on some disambiguations (true — osd) and false on others or perhaps false on all disambiguations (false — osd — only) or true — osd — only.

> The implications that preserve truth — oxd are those given by the first degree fragment of Priest's LP. Those that preserve both truth — osd and truth — osd — only are given by the first degree fragment of R — mingle. So we have two logics for ambiguous sentences — and lo, they are partly relevant. [25]

Lewis goes on to explain that a logic for ambiguity is needed for pessimists who do not believe that all sentences can be fully disambiguated before one applies one's logic. However, I do not think that Lewis has gone sufficiently far in making his case against relevance (as an important factor in truth preservation) for us to be persuaded to follow him on the road to developing a logic for equivocators, at least not in the context of programming an intelligent machine.

In the first place there is a problem with Lewis's account of the business of fragmentation. Lewis gives no details about how this process is actually carried out. He quite airily says that fragmentation of our beliefs is the result of the way our beliefs are used or the way they are stored. We might begin by agreeing that some sort of fragmentation does seem to operate on our total set of beliefs whenever we apply our minds to any particular subject. We seem to be capable of selecting for immediate attention only those pieces of information (only those beliefs) which are relevant to the project which is occupying our minds at any given moment. Thus if we are trying to figure out why the cabbages in our garden are suffering from leaf mould we call to mind all the information at our disposal on that particular aspect of gardening. Or if we are asked the way to Nassau Street we seem to be able to select for consideration a small amount of the total information about the street layout of the city which we have at our disposal. So fragmentation does seem to occur, but it seems to be controlled by some criterion of relevance. We fragment our total set of beliefs so that our working fragment contains (some of) what is relevant to the project in hand, whether that project be gardening or navigation.

The strident relevance logician says that it is only be taking relevance into account that we can preserve truth. In response, Lewis appears to be saying (correctly) that there are at least two distinct phases we go through when doing a piece of reasoning. The first phase is the selection of the premises — Lewis calls this phase fragmentation. The second phase is the deduction from the premises. Fragmentation is supposed to preserve truth without recourse tao relevance, but if I am right and fragmentation is carried out on the basis of criterion of relevance then the door is reopened for the relevance logician to claim that truth cannot be assuredly preserved unless relevance is taken into account, although now relevance would enter at a different phase of the reasoning process than was first suspected.

The second objection we might make to establishing the sort of logic for ambiguity which Lewis has in mind instead of taking relevance into account is that, even at best, it does n ot do any more than merely preserve truth. As we have seen above, humans, by contrast, do reason in such a way as to preserve relevance as well as truth. We would require an intelligent machine to pay attention to the relevance of the conclusions it drew to the premises it was working from. So there appears to be some justification for programming computers with a relevance logic or at the very least with the ability to subdivide their database into fragments on the basis of relevance to particular projects.

This raises the question of what logic is supposed to be doing or, more directly, what logic is. In the distance past it was thought that (classical) logic was a perfect representation of human reasoning, or at the very least an ideal against which to measure human reasoning. There is good reason to suppose that classical logic is neither of these things. It certainly does not represent a good model of the way humans actually reason — since it loses deductive selectivity when faced with contradictions. Insofar as classical logic is unconcerned with considerations of relevance and is limited to deductive reasoning it can hardly be thought of as an idealization of reason.

Lewis's attempt to avoid taking relevance into account at all does not look as if it can be of any help to us in trying to find a logic which would be suitable for an intelligent artifact, for in programming such a machine we are forced to take relevance into account at least at the stage of fragmentation and probably at the stage of deduction as well. Lewis has argued against various ways of trying to make good the claim that a sentence can be both true and false; the claim which underlies many of the recent attempts at many-valued (paraconsistent) logics. For an intelligent artifact we require both relevance and paraconsistency but there is no reason why we should expect both these aims to be satisfied by a logic. It seems to me that we should continue to praise relevance for its own sake and not because it might help with truth preservation. I have no idea what procedures might enable a computer to split its database into fragments relevant to particular projects at the sort of speed and with the degree of versatility which would be necessary for effective reasoning. I imagine that the problem is more appropriately the preserve of the computer scientist with experience in database management than of the logician. The overall aim would be to find an efficient way of:

(a) identifying what the project (context) is in a given situation;
(b) identifying which data are relevant to that project; and
(c) 'tagging' the data so that they can be retrieved for use when appropriate.

This would primarily apply to the first phase of reasoning. In the second phase humans seem very efficiently to zero in on relevant conclusions; we do not apparently come up with solutions and then test them for relevance. I imagine this is partly explained by our having some idea at the start of a piece of ordinary reasoning what the solution will look like. Thus if the problem before us is to get to the top of a hill, likely solutions will not include digging a tunnel. Occasionally, this preconception turns out to be very inaccurate and can prevent the discovery of the correct solution. Thus if we believe at the outset that no problem of astronomy will have an answer which involves the earth orbiting the sun, we are likely to have difficulty in answering questions which otherwise are quite simple. However, getting relevance included in the second phase of reasoning, as with the first phase, does not seem to be a problem for logicians. Thus we are free to concentrate on inconsistency.

Establishing a paraconsistent logic for an intelligent machine is not a particularly difficult problem of itself. However, as we have seen, making sense of the central claim of the available paraconsistent logics has proved to be a stumbling block. In the next section I will outline a logic for use in situations where consistency is not to be expected, let alone guaranteed, and which does not depend on the controversial claim that some sentences might be both true and false.

5.4   A LOGIC FOR INTELLIGENT ARTIFACTS

The central notion which we shall employ in the development of a logic for intelligent machines is the database. In actual computers, databases take a variety of physical forms. A typical database might be a collection of micro-chips storing electrical patterns which may be converted into binary code and (eventually) into numbers or letters, depending on the needs of the particular program. In the computer on which I am now working the letter 'a' is represented by the hexadecimal code 97_{16}, which is stored as 10010111_2

and which means that there is a location inside the chips of the computer where a pattern of higher and lower voltages of the following form is stored: high–low–low—high–low–high–high–high. However, 'a' could be stored in a different database quite differently. As Searle has observed, computers are not confined to the physical forms which we are used to but might be constructed from piles of stones and rolls of toilet paper. In such a computer 'a' might be stored as a sequence of small and large stones, or as an amount of stones, or yet again as a certain weight of stones. So when we talk about the database of a computer we will not be concerned with the particular physical realization which the database might take but only with the propositional content of the database. The database may profitably be thought of as the set whose members are the propositions stored by any arbitrary computer.

Let L be a propositional language whose set of propositional variables is P. Let v: P→{in, out} (i.e. v is an evaluation of the propositional variables.) A database D is specified by a valuation of the propositional variables. Suppose L has just three propositional variables Q, R, S, and v: Q→{in}, v: R→{in}, v: S→{out}. D will then be {Q, R}.

Let us now extend the propositional language to include the negations of propositions. We reason as follows:

A   NEGATION

t   If A is in the database −A will not be in the classical extention of the database.

f   If −A is in the database then A will not be in the classical extension of the database.

1   If A is in the database −A will not be in the classical extension of the database. Since −A is in the database A will not be in the classical extension of the database.

0   Since A is not in the database and −A is not in the database neither A nor −A will be in the classical extension of the database.

This sort of reasoning yields the following table for negation:

−	
t	f
f	t
1	1
0	0

A B   CONJUNCTION

t t   If A is in the database and B is in the database then A & B will be in the classical extension of the database.

t f   If −B is in the database −(A & B) will be in the classical extension of the database.

t 1   If −B is in the database then −(A & B) will be in the classical extension of the database. But since A is in the database and B is in the database the A & B will be in the classical extension of the database.

t 0   Since B is not in the database A & B will not be in the classical extension of the database and since A is in the database and −B is not in the database −(A & B) will not be in the classical extension of the database.

f t   If −A is in the database then −(A &B) will be in the classical extension of the database.

f f   If −A is in the database then −(A & B) will be in the classical extension of the database.

f 1   If −A is in the database then −(A & B) will be in the classical extension of the database.

f 0   If −A is in the database then −(A & B) will be in the classical extension of the database.

1 t   If −A is in the database then −(A & B) will be in the classical extension of the database. But since A is in the database and B is in the database then A & B will be in the classical extension of the database.

1 f   If −B is in the database then −(A & B) will be in the classical extension of the database.

1 1   If −Al is in the database and −B is in the database then −(A & B) will be in the classical extension of the database. But since A is in the database and B is in the database then A & B will be in the classical extension of the database.

1 0   If −A is in the database then −(A & B) will be in the classical extension of the database.

0 t   Since A is not in the database A & B will not be in the classical extension of the database and since A is in the database and −B is not in the database −(A & B) will not be in the classical extension of the database.

0 f   If −B is in the database then −(A & B) will be in the classical extension of the database.

0 1   If −A is in the database then −(A & B) will be in the classical extension of the database.

0 0   Since A is not in the database and B is not in the database A & B will not be in the classical extension of the database and since −A is not in the database and −B is not in the database −(A & B) will not be in the classical extension of the database either.

This sort of reasoning yields the following table for conjunction:

&	t	f	1	0
t	t	f	1	0
f	f	f	f	f
1	1	f	1	f
0	0	f	f	0

A B   DISJUNCTION

t t   If A is in the database then A ∨ B will be in the classical extension of the database.

t f   If A is in the database then A ∨ B will be in the classical extension of the database.

t 1   If A is in the database then A ∨ B will be in the classical extension of the database.

t 0   If A is in the database then A ∨ B will be in the classical extension of the database.

f t   If B is in the database then A ∨ B will be in the classical extension of the database.

f f   If −A is in the database and −B is in the database then −(A ∨ B) will be in the classical extension of the database.

f 1   If −A is in the database and −B is in the database then −(A ∨ B) will be in the classical extension of the database but since B is in the database A ∨ B will be in the classical extension of the database.

f 0   If A is not in the database and B is not in the database then A ∨ B will not be in the classical extension of the database. And since −B is not in the database −(A ∨ B) will not be in the classical extension of the database.

1 t   If B is in the database then A ∨ B will be in the classical extension of the database.

1 f   If A is int he database A ∨ B will be in the classical extension of the database. If −A is in the database and −B is in the database then −(A ∨ B) will be in the classical extension of the database.

1 1   If A is in the database A ∨ B will be in the classical extension of the database. If −A is in the database and −B is in the database then −(A ∨ B) will be in the classical extension of the database.

1 0   If A is in the database then A ∨ B will be in the classical extension of the database.

0 t   If B is in the database then A ∨ B will be in the classical extension of the database.

0 f   If A is not in the database and B is not in the database then A ∨ B will not be in the classical extension of the database. If −A is not in the database −(A ∨ B) will not be in the classical extension of the database.

0 1   If B is in the database then A ∨ B will be in the classical extension of the database.

0 0   If A is not in the database and B is not in the database then A ∨ B will not be in the classical extension of the database. If −A is not in the database and −B is not in the database then −(A ∨ B) will not be in the classical extension of the database.

This sort of reasoning leads to the following table for disjunction:

∨	t	f	1	0
t	t	t	t	t
f	t	f	1	0
1	t	f	1	t
0	t	0	t	0

A B   MATERIAL IMPLICATION

t t   If A is in the database and B is in the database then A ⇒ B will be in the classical extension of the database.

t f   If A is in the database and −B is in the database then −(A ⇒ B) will be in the classical extension of the database.

t 1   If A is in the database and B is in the database then A ⇒ B will be in the classical extension of the database. If A is in the database and −B is in the database then −(A ⇒ B) will be in the classical extension of the database.

t 0   If B is not in the database then A ⇒ B will not be in the classical extension of the database. If −B is not in the database then −(A ⇒ B) will not be in the database.

f t   If B is in the database then A ⇒ B will be in the classical extension of the database.

f f   If −A is in the database and −B is in the database then A ⇒ B will be in the classical extension of the database.

f 1   If B is in the database then A ⇒ B will be in the classical extension of the database.

f 0   If −A is in the database then A ⇒ B will be in the classical extension of the database.

1 t   If B is in the database then A ⇒ B will be in the classical extension of the database.

1 f   If −A is in the database and −B is in the database then A ⇒ B will be in the classical extension of the database. If A is in the database and −B is in the database then −(A ⇒ B) will be in the classical extension of the database.

1 1   If −A is in the database and −B is in the database then A ⇒ B will be in the classical extension of the database. If A is in the database and −B is in the database then −(A ⇒ B) will be in the classical extension of the database.

1 0   If −A is in the database then A ⇒ B will be in the classical extension of the database.

0 t   If B is in the database then A ⇒ B will be in the classical extension of the database.

0 f   If B is not in the database then A ⇒ B will not be in the classical extension of the database. If A is not in the database and −A is not in the database then −(A ⇒ B) will not be in the classical extension of the database.

0 1   If B is in the database then A ⇒ B will be in the classical extension of the database.

0 0   If B is not in the database and −B is not in the database then A ⇒ B will not be in the classical extension of the database. If A is not in the database and −A is not in the database then −(A ⇒ B) will not be in the classical extension of the database.

This sort of reasoning leads to the following table:

⇒	t	f	1	0
t	t	f	1	0
f	t	t	t	t
1	t	t	t	t
0	t	0	t	0

It will be noted that this table is consistent with the usual convention (in classical logic) of letting $A \Rightarrow B =^{df} -(A \ \& \ -B)$.

To summarize, this gives us the following tables:

−		&	t	f	1	0	V	t	f	1	0	⇒	t	f	1	0
t	f	t	t	f	1	0	t	t	t	t	t	t	t	f	1	0
f	t	f	f	f	f	f	f	t	f	1	0	f	t	t	t	t
1	1	1	1	f	1	f	1	t	1	1	t	1	t	1	1	t
0	0	0	0	f	f	0	0	t	0	t	0	0	t	0	t	0

There are 16 possible sorts of inference between which we will find it useful to distinguish. They are as follows:

(1) From premises which take t to a conclusion which takes t.

(2) From premises which take t to a conclusion which takes f.
(3) From premises which take t to a conclusion which takes 1.
(4) From premises which take t to a conclusion which takes 0.
(5) From premises which take f to a conclusion which takes t.
(6) From premises which take f to a conclusion which takes f.
(7) From premises which take f to a conclusion which takes 1.
(8) From premises which take f to a conclusion which takes 0.
(9) From premises which take 1 to a conclusion which takes t.
(10) From premises which take 1 to a conclusion which takes f.
(11) From premises which take 1 to a conclusion which takes 1.
(12) From premises which take 1 to a conclusion which takes 0.
(13) From premises which take 0 to a conclusion which takes t.
(14) From premises which take 0 to a conclusion which takes f.
(15) From premises which take 0 to a conclusion which takes 1.
(16) From premises which take 0 to a conclusion which takes 0.

These represent 16 ways of expanding the computer's database. What is now required is that we should decide for each of these possible methods of expansion whether it is legitimate or not.

In classical logic this is a relatively straightforward exercise. The one thing we are trying to preserve in classical logic is truth. The classical logician is concerned only to avoid situations in which an argument moves from premises which are true to a conclusion which is false. This tunnel vision has the effect of legitimizing arguments proceeding from false premises to any conclusion whatever. Thus it is classically valid to argue from 'Paris both is and is not the capital of France' to 'David Anderson has two noses'. Non-logicians show a commendable degree of scepticism when faced with arguments of this kind.

At the very least the classical approach has the following virtues: it preserves what is most important in arguments (truth) and it shows what is wrong with working from premises which are false (they can lead to conclusions which are false) and in particular what is wrong with contradictions (they can never serve as reliable premisses). But the story with the present logic is entirely different. This logic apparently does not concern itself with the truth or falsity of premises and conclusions but only with the presence or absence of propositions and their negations from a given database. So it seems that the touchstone of this logic cannot be truth preservation. However, this is not quite the case.

Suppose for a moment that all the propositions in a database were assigned 't's and 'f's. In such circumstances there would be no harm in treating t as meaning 'true' and f as meaning 'false' and using classical logic. At least there would be no harm if it were not for the fact that an intelligent machine would have more ways of extending the content of its database than mere (classical) deductive reasoning. As we have seen, there would almost certainly be induction as well as sense input, reading, listening to others and so on. With these multifarious means of extending its database the computer is almost certain to corrupt its database, and even if Lewis-style fragmentation is utilized by the computer and the contradictions do not become obvious to the machine the presence of contradictions in the database might lead to a greater and greater number of falsehoods entering the database, being treated as true, and allowing yet more falsehoods into the database. this would lead to a 'breeding' of contradictions which would eventually completely corrupt the database.

The formal move of changing from reading t as 'true' to reading t as 'present in the database when −t is absent from the database — of moving from 'truth values' to prescence values does not directly prevent the corruptive effect of propositions which take 1 (i.e. contradiction); what it does is to make sense of the semantics underpinning the logic which the computer will use. The resulting logic should minimize the corruptive effect of propositions taking 1 (i.e. should inhibit the extension of the database to include propositions which currently take f).

It should be stressed that we are still concerned with truth. If a proposition takes t or 1 we may say that the computer believes it to be true (if the psychological language is a problem here we can replace 'believes A to be true' with 'will treat A as if A were true' and if a proposition takes f or 1 the computer believes the proposition to be false. We are still concerned to avoid a situation in which a database contains many falsehoods. The best way to do this is to attempt to inhibit the extension of the database to include propositions which currently take f.

With these introductory comments out of the way let's turn to the 16 types of inference outlined above and attempt to give some sort of a ruling on them.

Perhaps the first thing to draw attention to is that of the 16 types of inference outlined only eight will ever actually occur in any piece of reasoning. The computer will never argue from premisses which take f overall. The explanation for this is really quite simple. It is obvious that the computer can only reason from premisses which are in its database. If the premisses overall take an f this means that the presence values of the atoms are so distributed that one or more of the premisses individually takes an f and this in turn means that that particular premiss does not appear in the database. Since one of the premisses is not in the database it cannot be used as a premiss in an actual piece of reasoning.

Thus cases (5), (6), (7) and (8) will never occur and it will not (for the practical purpose of inhibiting the extension of the database to include propositions taking f) matter if we say that they are legitimate or illegitimate types of inference. If we, theoretically, allow inferences like cases (5), (6), (7) and (8) there will be more types of argument form allowable in the resulting system than otherwise. It is a positive bonus to have extra types of argument form available to the computer (so long as this is consistent with our attempt to avoid the corruption of the database) so we can feel happy in declaring (5), (6), (7) and (8) as legitimate types of inference. Similar comments apply to cases (13), (14), (15) and (16).

We have said that our aim of avoiding the corruption of the database is best served by not allowing the extension of the database to include propositions which take f. Let us put this into effect by declaring illegitimate cases (2) and (10). The other six cases we will declare legitimate. Formally:

> Let L be a propositional language whose set of propositional variables is P. Let $v:P\rightarrow\{t,f,1,0\}$ (i.e. v is an evaluation of the propositional variables). Let v^+ be the natural extension of v to all sentences of L using the above truth tables. If E is a set of sentences of L, we define:
>
> $E \vdash A$ iff there is no v such $v^+(A)=f$ but for all $B \in E$, $v^+(B)=t$ or 1.
>
> $\vdash A$ iff $0 \in A$ (i.e. for all v, $v^+(A)=t$ or 1).

For the sake of convenience we will call the logic just outlined LM (logic for machines). If an inference is legitimate within LM we will call it 'LM-valid', and otherwise the inference will be 'LM-invalid'. If the inference is LM-valid we will say that its premisses 'LM-entail' its conclusion. Let us now examine the way LM handles the key inferences which ran Priest's LP into trouble.

In the first place, we may note that LM meets the minimum requirement of a paraconsistent logic, that is to say it does not lose deductive selectivity when faced with a contradiction as a premiss. $A \& -A \vdash B$ is not LM-valid, because there is a distribution of presence values which designates B as f and $A \& -A$ as 1 (i.e. where B is f and A is 1).

Unfortunately this is not the only major departure which LM makes from the classical pattern of inference. Disjunctive syllogism is also LM-invalid. There is a possible distribution of presence values which has disjunctive syllogism going from premisses which (overall) take 1 to a conclusion which takes f. Thus $A, -A \vee B \vdash B$ fails when B takes f and A takes 1.

This would be tolerable if it were not that a number of important argument forms involving hook ($\Rightarrow$) are also LM-invalid:

$A \Rightarrow (B \& -B) \vdash -A$
is LM-invalid when A takes t and B takes 1

$A \Rightarrow B, \Rightarrow \vdash A \Rightarrow C$
is LM-invalid when A takes t, B takes 1, and C takes f

$A, A \Rightarrow B \vdash B$
is LM-invalid when A takes 1 and B takes f

$A \Rightarrow B, -B \vdash -A$
is LM-invalid when A takes t and B takes 1

Thus all the important inferences which were LP-invalid are also LM-invalid. This is hardly much of a surprise, but there are options open to LM which are closed to LP. You will recall that the main reason why LP was rejected was not that it was crippled in just those situations when it should have been most useful but that we could not make sense of a sentence being 'true and false'. It was no solution to Priest's difficulties for us to stipulate new truth tables for the logical operators of LP because of the underlying incoherence of the system's semantics. However, LM makes no commitment to sentences being true and false, so if we can stipulate new presence tables for some of the logical operators of LM we will have saved the system.

I propose that we rethink the table for '⇒', which currently is as follows:

⇒	t	f	1	0
t	t	f	1	0
f	t	t	t	t
1	t	1	1	t
0	t	0	t	0

There are quite a few alternative readings of '⇒' available (there are 16 places to fill in a four-valued presence table, each of which may take four different values, so there are a total of 4^{16} different presence tables, any one of which might be associated with '⇒') so rather than work through all of them to try to find an alternative let's see if we can make use of our intuitions about '⇒' to suggest a new semantics for it.

In the first place there doesn't seem to be anything wrong with the part of the table that deals with atoms which take only t or f. It seems in order to suggest that for the formula $A \Rightarrow B$ if the consequent is in the database then the whole formula should be in the classical extension of the database. The whole formula should also be in the classical extension in just those cases where the antecedent is not in the database. In no other situation should the whole formula be in the classical extension of the database. This would provide a very strong form of '⇒', which would be defined by the following table:

⇒	t	f	1	0
t	t	f	f	f
f	t	t	t	t
1	t	f	f	f
0	t	f	f	f

We will call the system of logic which has '⇒' so defined and all the other operators defined as they are in LM, as well as having the same conditions for entailment as LM, LM^1. Let's look at the way LM^1 treats the sort of argument forms which caused LP and LM so much trouble.

$$A \& -A \vdash B$$

is LM^1-invalid when A takes 1 and B takes f. So the system does not lose deductive selectivity in the face of contradictions.

$$A, -A \lor B \vdash B$$

is LM^1-invalid when A takes 1 and B takes f.

These results were expected since LM^1 has the same semantics for '&' and '∨' as LM.

$$A \Rightarrow (B \& -B) \vdash -A$$

is LM^1-valid. This can be shown as follows: for the argument form to be LM^1-invalid the conclusion would have to take f and the premisses (overall) t or 1. If −A takes f then A must take t. There is no distribution of presence values which will assign A ⇒ (B & −B) a t or 1 (overall) when A takes t. So the argument form must be LM^1-valid.

$$A ⇒ B, B ⇒ C ⊢ A ⇒ C$$

is LM^1-valid. For the premisses to take t (overall) A ⇒ B must take t and B ⇒ C must take t. For A ⇒ B to take t either A must take f or B must take t, but A cannot take f or A ⇒ C would take t (and *ex hypothesi* it takes f), so B must take t., If B ⇒ C is to take t (overall) and B takes t, then C must take t as well. Thus if the premisses (overall) take t then C must take t and if C takes t then A ⇒ C must also take t.

For the premisses to take 1 (overall) either both A ⇒ B and B ⇒ C must take 1 or one of them must take t while the other takes 1. But there is no distribution of presence values which allows either premiss to take 1, so the argument form must be LM^1-valid.

$$A, A ⇒ B ⊢ B$$

is LM^1-valid. For the premisses (overall) to take t each of the premisses must individually take t. So A takes t but, *ex hypothesi*, B must take f.

If the premisses (overall) take 1, at least one of the premisses must individually take 1. We know that no distribution of presence values will assign 1 to A ⇒ B, so A must take 1 individually. We also know that B takes f, so A ⇒ B must take f. This means that the premisses (overall) take f.

$$A ⇒ B, −B ⊢ −A$$

is LM^1-valid. For the premisses (overall) to take t each of the premisses must individually take t. For −B to take t, B must take f. If B takes f, then the only way A ⇒ B can take f is if A takes f. However, we know that −A takes f and hence that A takes t.

For the premisses (overall) to take 1, at least one of the premisses must individually take 1. We know that no distribution of presence values will assign a 1 to A⇒B, so −B must take 1. Thus B must take 1 and since *ex hypothesi* −A takes f, A must take t, thus A ⇒ B must take f, and hence the premisses overall must take f.

LM^1 also preserves ∨ − introduction, & − introduction and & − elimination as well as retaining the inter-definition, A ∨ B =^{df} −(−A & −B). This all combines to make LM^1 a very powerful system for reasoning in an environment where the presence of contradictions is almost unavoidable.

6

Living with computers

6.1 INTRODUCTION

So far, I have argued for the claim that computers may eventually be able to perform all the tasks which humans can perform and that they may be able to perform these tasks as well or better than humans can. This represents an important conclusion in its own right, but I think that much more can in fact be said on behalf of computers. I now propose to argue that computers can properly be thought of as an emergent life form, that living computers would have genuine interests and would be entitled to press moral claims against each other and against humans.

6.2 DISTINGUISHING LIFE FROM NON-LIFE

Obviously, a prerequisite for any attempt to argue that the set of living things should be extended to include a new member (where that new member significantly differs from any of the existing members) is that an examination be carried out of the criteria for life.

> Whenever we find a new phenomenon which partakes to some degree of the nature of those which we have already termed 'living phenomena' but does not conform to all the associated aspects which define the term 'life' we are faced with the problem whether to enlarge the word 'life' so as to include them, or to define it in a more restrictive way so as to exclude them. [1]

We are forced to ask what life is or, a little less drastically, what distinguishes living things from non-living things.

In what follows I will outline a number of the distinctions which various researchers have thought it worth drawing between life and non-life, and in total this will constitute an attempt to draw up criteria for life, which can then be matched against computers to see if they might qualify as living things.

6.2.1 Resistance to decay

Many attempts have been made to list the criteria for life. Berrill takes growth, metabolism, autonomous movement and self-replication as the essential functions of life [2].

Michael Ovenden characterizes living things as having the ability to maintain their structure and to resist decay [3]; this theme is echoed by Konrad Lorenz, who describes life as 'a steady state of enormous general improbability' [4], and Norbert Weiner who says that life forms 'tend for a time to maintain and often even to increase the level of their organization, as a local enclave in the general stream of increasing entropy' [5].

The general theme running through each of these comments is a reading of the second law of thermodynamics which (in the present case) is understood as saying that the environment tends to disrupt the structure and organization of everything there is. Life forms are thought of as sharing the feature of being able to (temporarily) resist this process of decay. But this does not appear to be a characteristic unique to living things. After all, no one supposes for a moment that stones are alive but they apparently manage to maintain their level of organization in the face of a disruptive environment with much greater success than most acknowledged life forms. A human being moves from conception through maturity and decay into death in a much shorter period of time than is required for a stone to be worn down to dust by the action of the environment.

It might be argued that despite outward appearances to the contrary stones are in fact in a state of (very slow) decay. Stones might never succeed in maintaining their structure in the face of their environment. But such an argument would not apply to, say, the formation of crystals. The basic material out of which crystals are formed is, in the first instance, relatively unstructured and unorganized. With the formation of the crystal the basic material actually manages to increase its level of organization (a decrease in entropy) and this structure may well be maintained for a very long period before (inevitable) decay and loss of structure results.

6.2.2   Feeding: processing energy to forestall entropy
There is a feature shared by all life forms which Sayre draws attention to:

> ... the rather remarkable fact that living organisms alone among small scale natural systems are able to receive energy from other systems existing thermodynamically at lower energy levels. [6]

That is to say that life forms feed. The actual process is quite astounding because in accordance with the second law of thermodynamics the total amount of entropy in the combined system of an organism and its immediate environment increases as a result of the process of digestion. However, if the organism is considered in isolation, a net decrease in entropy is observed.

> In some way the living organism is able to slough off the entropy resulting from interaction with its environment. [7]

This ability to process energy characterizes all life forms from micro-organisms to elephants but, as with the ability to avoid entropy in a disruptive environment, processing energy is not unique to life forms. A solar cell processes energy, as does a windmill. But unlike life forms, windmills and solar cells do not avoid entropy by processing energy. The entropy of a solar cell or a windmill increases as it operates.

6.2.3 Autonomous movement

As we have noted already Berrill takes the property of automomous movement to be fundamental to all life forms. Simons argues that:

> Our cactus, for example, may not appear to have much autonomous movement — from which we are not expected to conclude that the cactus is not alive. [8]

Of course, this misses the point. A cactus does display autonomous movement and this is manifested in at least two main ways. Like all plants, cacti will incline toward the direction of their primary light source. Thus if a cactus is placed in a laboratory and light is shone from one position only, the cactus will eventually 'lean' towards the light source.

The second way in which the automomous movement of the cactus is made manifest is during growth. As a cactus matures it pushes out root growth below the surface as well as the more familiar growth above the surface. Of course, both these sorts of autonomous movement are, in the nature of things, painstakingly slow by human standards, and the casual observer might be forgiven for failing to notice them, but that does not detract from the fact that even cacti display autonomous movement.

However, there is some substance to the point behind Simon's comment. We can perfectly well imagine a life form which after its initial period of growth made no further movement of any kind. We would not be inclined to say that this creature was dead (or even inanimate), at least not so long as there were other criteria available for deciding when it was, in fact, dead. We might initially decide that it was alive on the basis of observations of its initial period of growth and this might be supplemented by observations of its metabolism and its ultimate decay.

However, there are limits to the degree of exception we are prepared to tolerate to the principle that all life forms exhibit autonomous movement. In the present case, the life form in question has a history of autonomous movement (its period of growth). In the period of its life cycle during which it does not move at all we are able to call on supplementary evidence for the existence of life. The fact that we need to call on other evidence is indicative of the universality of autonomous movement among life forms.

When an acknowledged life form stops moving (for good) we have strong prima facie evidence that the life form has expired. When something has never moved we have strong *prima facie* evidence that it is inanimate.

If it turns out that not all life forms are capable of autonomous movement (although this seems unlikely) might it still be true to say that only life forms are capable of autonomous movement? If so, then no further argument would be needed to establish that some machines are alive. For example, we might rig a photo-electric cell to a toy truck controlled by some very simple micro-circuitry which would move the truck forward in conditions of strong light, backwards in conditions of weak light and which would stop the truck in conditions of darkness. Now such a truck would show at least as much autonomy of movement as a mature daffodil, and like a daffodil the truck's movements would be related to light sensitivity. The movements of the truck would have to be regarded as autonomous because they would not have been predetermined by some programmer, at least they would have only been predetermined in the same very general way that a daffodil's movement is predetermined by its microstructure — all daffodils are light-sensitive, and will move in ways a, b, c, ... in light conditions, 1, 2, 3, ..., etc. The person who makes the truck and who writes the program has no more idea of precisely where the truck will be at any precise moment in the future than the gardener has of the exact angle his daffodil will be standing at any given moment. Of course both gardener and programmer will have an approximate idea of the positions in question but cannot do better than this for the actual positions of the truck and daffodil depend on factors which are out of the programmer's/gardener's control.

Thus we are forced to take the same stance toward the movement of daffodils as we do towards the truck; either both display autonomous movement or neither does. This being so, we are left to decide what importance we wish to attach to autonomous movement. It seems likely that autonomous movement is a necessary condition for being a life form but in the light of the truck example it would be surprising if many people felt willing to count autonomous movement as a sufficient condition for being alive.

6.2.4 Reproduction

Life forms are very good at reproducing themselves. So much so that there is a temptation to say that the ability to reproduce is a necessary condition for being alive. But here, as almost everywhere else, nature confounds us. There are plenty of human beings who cannot reproduce and yet we feel no inclination to say that they are any less alive for that. Perhaps we might think of these people as being somehow defective and maintain that while certain individual life forms may lack the ability to reproduce the types of life form of which they are examples must have the ability to reproduce in order to count as being alive.

This response would sound odd even if it were not for creatures like the worker bee, which are living examples of its falsity. After all worker bees cannot reproduce at all, this function being performed by queen bees alone. Certain sorts of cells cannot reproduce (for example, human brain cells) but are still thought of as forming living tissue.

The situation is further complicated by the sheer variety of ways of bringing about reproduction, which may lead to some difficulty in saying what reproduction actually is.

Mammals generally set reproduction in motion by transferring sperm from the male into the female. Precise methods differ but close physical contact is necessary in all cases. However, this is only one option.

Many animals reproduce outside their bodies and thus avoid physical contact at all, for example female freshwater fish start reproduction by laying eggs onto a riverbed and the male comes along and sprays sperm over the eggs, which are then buried.

To carry the process a stage further, some life forms use a third party (from a different species) to aid reproduction. Thus it is the bees are employed by a variety of flora to spread their pollen, and human gardeners perform much the same function.

Not all life forms can even be divided neatly into male and female. Trees are on the whole strictly unisex. They perform reproduction without dividing into pairs, although they do often rely on animals, or the elements to spread their seed.

Thus it is that reproduction is not a uniform process; it may or may not involve physical contact between the male and female of a species. It might involve one, two or more individuals which may or may not be of the same species. It can be carried on inside an adult or outside, nearby or at a distance. There are species all of whose members can reproduce equally well (oak trees) and some in which there exist classes of members who cannot reproduce at all (worker bees).

6.2.5   Feedback: responding to the environment

Sayre points to a feature which is shared by all life forms:

> Life, in contrast with even the most persistent whirlpool, tornado or nuclear explosion, is a process of a highly organised and stable system. This means that life depends for its unusual entropic characteristics upon the interaction of many parts of an operating system, maintained in adjustment by negative feedback mechanisms. [9]

Feedback is one of the basic concepts involved in cybernetics. We might begin by thinking of feedback as falling into two categories: positive and negative. According to Sayre, positive feedback 'is a source of instability leading if unchecked to the destruction of the system itself'. Everyone who has owned a house for a number of years will have seen positive feedback in action. In the face of the agents of erosion the walls develop small cracks which then allow rain to enter. In winter the rain freezes and in expanding cracks the walls further, thus allowing even more rain to get in and so on until either the house falls down or repairs are made. Sayre gives the example of gunpowder, which . . .

> explodes because the chemical combination of its components produces heat, which increases the rate of combination with resultant increase of heat, and so forth, issuing in the (only apparently) instantaneous destruction of the combining elements. [10]

Further examples could be given but the common feature which identifies them all as examples of positive feedback is an 'increase in the rate of intensity of a pattern of activity resulting from the performance of the activity itself' [11]. The feedback is called 'positive' because 'such a process results in self-administered positive reinforcement of the activity in question' [12].

If positive feedback leads to instability and loss of control, the opposite might reasonably be expected from negative feedback, and such is the case, Negative feedback acts to prevent 'excessive deviation of the system from a standard operating condition'. For example, I have short eyesight and wear spectacles. For summer driving, I have a pair of glasses which utilize a sort of negative feedback. The glasses in question are photochromic, that is to say that as light falling on the glass gets brighter the glasses respond by getting darker, and vice versa. Thus the spectacles keep the brightness of light falling on my eyes within an acceptable (i.e. fairly restricted) range.

Using a similar example Sayre introduces the notion of a 'feedback loop':

> A clear illustration of negative feedback is the process by which the level of illumination is regulated on the retina. When retinal excitation increases beyond a certain optimal level, the pupil of the eye contracts to decrease the amount of incoming light energy; conversely, the pupil dilates to admit more light when the excitation level decreases, in the circuit of interactions the rods and the cones of the retina serve the visual system as sensors for detecting current levels of illumination in the environment, the neutal mechanisms that summate retinal stimulation serve as information processors, and the pupiliary muscles that shape the aperture serve as effectors maintaining the system in a constant operating state. This combination of sensors, information processors and effectors constitutes what we will call a 'feedback loop'. [13]

Organisms as simple as bacteria cells have been found to utilize such feedback loops. However, it appears yet again that even though all life forms appear to have the utilization of negative feedback mechanisms in common it is not only life forms which use negative feedback.

Feedback (of all kinds) can be thought of as responding to the environment and there are all sorts of inanimate things which respond to their environment. I have already given the example of sunglasses; we could add thermostats, barometers, automatic doors and many more.

6.2.6   Finding life: the systems approach

All life forms can be thought of as being systems which have subsystems and parts. For example, a tree is a system, its roots, bark, and foliage are all subsystems and its individual cells are parts. Any life form which uses a feedback loop (i.e. any life form) can always be analysed as having at least three sorts of subsystem: sensors, processors and effectors. The actual stuff out of which the life form is made can always be analysed as being the 'parts'. Under such an analysis it is clear that life forms, like non-life forms, are made from parts which are inanimate.

Thus life does not seem to be a property of the parts of a life form when viewed as parts but is a property of the parts of a life form when viewed as a system. There is a clear parallel between this situation in biology and the situation which is found in the philosophy of mind when we attempt to locate consciousness. It will be recalled that the failure to seriously take account of this point was one of the weaknesses of John Searle's criticism of artificial intelligence. When considering Searle I concluded that digital computers could have consciousness and that the 'Chinese room' example did nothing to indicate otherwise, and now I propose to argue that digital computers (with modification and improvement) could count as life forms and that the computers with which we are so familiar today should therefore be regarded as emergent life forms.

6.3 COMPUTERS AS LIFE FORMS

Much of what I have said so far in this section has been an attempt to find some essential feature which is shared by all life forms and is absent from all non-life forms. This attempt has been a failure but that is hardly a surprise. The problem with establishing criteria for life is that they must be sufficiently flexible to encompass all the life forms from a simple virus to a human being and sufficiently tight to exclude all non-life forms. No single feature has emerged which could serve as the criterion for life, nor has any particular group of such features been identifed which could serve as criteria.

What has come out of out discussion so far is the likelihood that the interesting features which we have noted in some life forms might be like the individual characteristics that go to make up a family likeness. That is to say all life forms must have at least some of these features but there is no single feature or particular subset of features which a life form must have in order to count as being alive.

There are two questions which we must now pose: in the first place, could any computer be designed which had all of the features which we have so far drawn attention to (thereby ensuring that the machine has all the important features which we have characterized as distinguishing life from non-life), and in the second place, given that such a machine could be manufactured would we be right to say that it was alive?

6.3.1 Resisting decay

Metal is as prone to decay and damage as flesh and, left unattended, robots would steadily increase in entropy until they simply fell apart. However, we can easily imagine a robot which had the facility for carrying out repairs to itself. Suppose that a robot engaged in painting car bodies got its painting arm crushed in an accident. There might easily be some extra programming given to the robot in order to enable it to stop what it was doing and report to a repair centre where other (medical) robots could repair the damage. Small problems, like burned out resistors, might be handled by the unaided robot. It might carry a selection of spares which it might fit at the appropriate moment. Spots of rust could be given an anti-rust treatment as the need arose. In this sort of way a robot might resist decay.

Of course, the techniques for resisting decay which I have outlined are rather different from those used by any of the life forms with which we are daily familiar. The main difference lies in the degree to which (say) human resistance to decay seems to be self-dependent. While humans do go to hospitals to have defective parts of their body repaired or replaced it is also true to say that this does not represent the normal method by which they resist decay. People simply do not go around with little first aid kits containing spare skin cells which they laboriously stick on in place of old dead skin cells.

However, I chose to suggest that robots might avoid decay in the way I did in order to makle clearer the point that the techniques employed for resisting decay are not all that important. I could have suggested that robots be made of a material which has the ability to regenerate whenever an electric charge of a certain strength is passed through it (presumably by a process something like electrolysis). However, I did not think that this was necessary. When we considered the ability of life forms to resist decay, it did not seem appropriate to consider techniques, the important thing was that all life forms seem to be able to resist entropy, and so it is here.

6.3.2 Feeding

Earlier we characterized feeding as processing energy in order to forestall entropy. A computer analogue of feeding might be achieved by a machine which plugged itself into the nearest power outlet whenever its batteries were beginning to run down. Once more I have deliberately chosen a fairly contrived method of feeding for computers, because the precise means by which computers process energy just seems irrelevant. Other possibilities are open to computers: perhaps they could be fitted with solar power and draw their energy direct from the sun, if this seems too alien computers might be fitted with conversion units (like stomachs) which enabled them to reclaim some of the energy latent in scrap materials, or they could be made completely independent of humans by enabling them to make use of some naturally occurring material like grass or chickweed. The exact method by which computers manage to process energy is not so important as the fact that they do manage it.

6.3.3 Autonomous movement

There is no real difficulty in making a computer which is capable of autonomous movement. There are a variety of ways in which this has already been achieved. One need look no further than the thousands of industrial robots which are now in existence. Autonomous movement could equally well be said to be present in a machine fitted to a solar cell and programmed to move (slowly) in the direction of any available light source.

In life forms we observed that two sorts of autonomous movement could be distinguished. The first was the sort of physical transportation of the whole organism within the environment, while the second was internal to the organism and was typified by growth. On the face of it it might seem impossible to get a machine which actually grew but this is not so. Admittedly it would be more difficult to arrange matters so that a machine grew than it would be to get it to move around its environment, but there are at least two ways in which this might be achieved.

First, a machine might be made from a substance which tends to add layers to itself in the presence of sunshine. In this way a machine would gradually grow as it aged. Secondly, we might program a machine to move about its environment in search of materials out of which to build itself new parts, which it could then add on and thereby grow. Once again I have chosen a couple of fairly contrived methods by which a machine might do what life forms do. But the techniques utilizied by life forms are very diverse and there is no reason why machines should not add to them.

The adding on of spare parts is not as unusual as it might sound; it might, after all, just be thought of as being another sort of metamorphosis, and many creatures have a protective outer layer which grows and sheds layers from time to time.

6.3.4 Feedback

In outlining how machines might forestall entropy, feed and achieve autonomous movement, I have already given a number of examples of machines responding to their environment. In this way machines once again mirror naturally occurring life forms.

As a machine searches its environment (autonomous movement) for a power outlet into which to plug itself (feeding) to prevent its batteries running down (resisting entrophy) it is interacting with its environment, and this whole process seems to be an example of negative feedback because it leads to the maintenance of stability and control. We can identify the feedback loop: the sensors are the parts of the computer which (a) detect power drain and (b) test the environment for the presence of a power outlet; the processors are represented by the chips of the computer; the effectors are the wheels which move the machine about and the arm which plugs itself into the power source.

6.3.5 Autonomy again

There are two related worries which occur to most people as they are presented with the arguments in favour of computers as a life form which I have just outlined. The first concerns the degree to which computer movement/growth can be seriously thought of as being 'autonomous'. The problem appears to be that computers can only do what their programs tell them to do and so any movement which they might exhibit is not autonomous but is dictated by the outside agency of the programmer — computers can never be free. The second, and clearly related, quibble is that computers are not 'naturally' occurring like diffodils or dogs and so cannot really be life forms at all.

Let's deal with these worries in turn. The first objection has two elements. On the one hand there is the complaint that computer movement is not autonomous because it depends on programs and programmers. It seems to me that this misunderstands either what is meant by autonomous or the role of programmers. The movement of a machine is autonomous just when it is cotrolled from within the machine alone and does not depend from moment to moment on the exercise of control from an outside agency. The program which directs the movements of the machine is part of the machine. Just as there is no merit in trying to portray the human mind as an outside force which controls the human body, there is no merit in trying to construe a program as an outside agency which controls a machine although, like the rest of the parts of the machine, it is put there by an external agent. It is possible to misunderstand the role of the programmer in the following sort of way: the machine's movements are controlled by the programmer because he has predetermined what all of its movements are going to be. Strangely enough this sort of objection never seems to arise in connection with (say) flowers. A flower is a relatively simple device (at least as far as autonomous movement is concerned). For the purposes of this discussion we can think of all its adult movements as being governed by the simple instruction 'Incline towards the brightest available light source'. There is no question of a flower being free in the way humans seem to be; it may be thought of as following a program which puts this single instruction into effect, and the instructions (genetic coding) which actually control the flower were put in it by the outside agency of evolutionary forces acting on its ancestors. Yet no-one feels inclined to argue that the movements of a flower are anything other than autonomous. Perhaps it is because the outside force which supplied the 'program' was itself a naturally occurring phenomenon. My reply to this is that human programmers are naturally occurring phenomena and as such may be thought of as being the machine analogue of the forces of evolution acting on a flower's ancestors.

Perhaps it might still be objected that the forces of evolution do not 'intend' to produce the effects that they do but merely produce them. Programmers intentionally write the programs they do and this somehow makes all the difference. Such an argument does not cut much ice. I would contend that animals eat the plants they do through choice — they intend to eat them. Further that animals complete with their intentions are an evolutionary force and that as a result it would be mistaken to think of the intentions of a programmer as being something really out of the ordinary. If this does not convince, then think of the role that human gardeners play in the development of new plants. There is no justification for thinking of there being a great difference in the intentions of gardeners and those of program-mers — both are a perfectly ordinary evolutionary force.

It should not concern us when we are considering how far computers can be thought of as exhibiting autonomous movement how the computer came to be as it is but only whether, given that it is, the movement which it displays is effected solely from within or depends on some outside agency. I contend that computers could be developed to exhibit truly autonomous movement.

The second worry which arises — computers are not naturally occurring so cannot be life forms — has already, to some extent, been covered. The basic point underlying my reply here is the same as for the first problem and is one of the fundamental attitudes upon which the whole of this book is built) — we should deal with computers on their own individual merits and should not concern ourselves in this instance with their ancestry. Imagine we found a candidate life form on another planet and after all our tests had been carried out we were prepared to grant that, at last, extra-terrestrial life had been uncovered. It strikes me as absurd that anyone should want to withdraw the ascription of life from this creature just because archaeological excavation later uncovered documents which showed beyond a shadow of doubt that a past civilization on that planet had in fact brought the creature into existence.

Most of the world's religions claim that man was created by God, just as the creature on the planet was created by a now extinct civilization. Among the many objections raised to this view of man's genesis which I have encountered I have yet to read that creation implies that we are not actually alive. The case for a computer's not being alive by virtue of its having been made by human beings also has still to be made.

6.3.6 Reproduction

Reproduction should pose no more of a problem for machines than any of the other features which we have so far considered. Not so long ago there was an advertising campaign run by a car manufacturer which showed a picture of the latest model of car complete with the caption 'HAND-BUILT BY ROBOTS'. The tendency for machines to be used semi-autonomously to build other machines is already well established. It does not require a great leap of the imagination to conceive of fully autonomous robots producing other fully autonomous robots.

Of course as the example stands we do not have reproduction like human reproduction but something which more closely resembles cloning. After all, the worker robots do not pass on any of their features to their offspring. However, this does not pose any problem. We can imagine two (or more) robots sitting down and discussing which features to incorporate in the next robot off the production line. Perhaps the traditional arm mechanism is inefficient and needs to be altered, maybe the new robot should be sensitive to ultraviolet light, and so on.

This whole unfamiliar process is no more outlandish than humans going along to their doctor and examining the genes of test tube fertilized embryos in order to pick one which does not have mental or physical disability or even eyes of a colour which displeases the parents, and so on. The human case is almost within our grasp and whatever our moral stance towards it, I doubt if anyone would be inclined to argue that it did not represent a case of genuine reproduction.

There are several reasons why people do not take the same view about the robot case. In the first place the robots do not seem to contribute anything other than opinions and labour to the reproduction process. Describing the robots as parents would be like describing the doctors, nurses, and laboratory staff as parents in the test tube example. The thing that marks out parents as parents is the contribution of a part of themselves to the reproductive process. Once the sperm and ovum have been supplied the identity of the parents is fixed; anyone is free to alter the genetic features of the fertilized egg but their input, however extensive, will not amount to parenthood.

I appreciate this objection but I do not share it. I suspect that the notion of reproduction is sufficiently flexible to cope with the computer case. However, if others do not share my opinion then perhaps the following amendment will satisfy. We can imagine each robot being designed so that it has a small number of blank EPROMs (electronically programmable read-only memory chips) inserted into its chest. Over the period of the robot's life we may imagine parts of its accumulated experience being recorded on these chips. When the time comes for robots to reproduce they go along to the insemination factory, where a single EPROM is removed from each parent and used to form the basis of the new robot's brain. The finished robot is in turn fitted with a number of blank EPROMs. In this case robots actually contribute a physical part of themselves to the repoduction process, and this contribution is not idle for it serves to pass on features of the parents to the child.

Another commonly raised objection to regarding the above example as a genuine case of reproduction is the degree to which the robots appear to be parasitic on their environment in general and human beings in particular. The metal out of which the robots are formed has to be mined and processed rather than simply grown like flesh. I confess to finding this objection somewhat difficult to comprehend. It is as if the obector believes that the process of growing arms and legs from a fertilized ovum was independent of the outside world. This transformation can only take place because materials from outside the mother (food) are processed and passed onto the embryo, which in turn processes the material and makes flesh and bone out of it. There is no difference of principle involved in going out to the environment and mining ore which is then processed and taken, as metal, to an insemination factory and finally utilized as part of a new living creature. To be sure, the scales are different and the precise methods differ, but in the human case just as with the robot materials which are external to both partners and child alike are gathered, processed and utilized.

The vital role which human beings may (or may not) play in this whole affair changes nothing. Suppose that the ore gathering, the metal making, the micro-chip production and even the programming were done by human beings — though it should be understood that, in fact, none of these activities need actually pass outside the control of properly programmed robots — then nothing would be changed. All of the materials which humans traditionally ate were to some extent the product of the labours of other living creatures. Indeed, much of our food was (and is) either itself a living creature or the seed of a living creature. We do not think of this dependence on other creatures for raw materials as compromising our right to describe ourselves as genuinely reproducing so why should we take a different attitude toward machine reproduction?

6.3.7   Conclusion

We recognize life across a wide variety of life forms. At one end there are viruses, microbes and cells while at the other we have cats, horses and human beings. It is exceptionally difficult to develop a definition of 'life' because of the flexibility which such a definition would be required to have. It is important also to make sure that the definition does not become so flexible so as to include as living things like stones which are not in fact alive.

One way to tackle this problem is to try to establish criteria for life, but we noticed that problems arose here too. In the first place the features which seemed at first to be universal to life forms often turned out to be not so universal as we had hoped. The characteristics which we ended up with were hardly the sort of thing which the ordinary man thinks of when he says 'my cat is alive'. For each of the characteristics we identified it was possible to think of an example of a non-life form which had that characteristic.

We took the view that we might be dealing with a 'family resemblance' criterion for life and the response to this was to present an example of a machine which exemplified all of the criteria for life which we had been able to identify. Such a machine would appear to have an irresistible claim to be a life form. I take the view that this claim should not be resisted; however, if anyone cannot happily accommodate the idea of a living machine then let him suggest further critera which do not exclude recognized life forms or likely future additions to the class of living things (for example, extra-terrestrial life) and which are incapable of being exemplified by a machine.

The creature which I argued for in the early parts of this book was capable of not only thinking as well as a human being but of exactly reproducing all of our behaviour. I appreciate that if I were to open a door in my chest and reveal a mass of circuitry some people might still want to claim that (a) I had never been able to mentate but only to artificially signal and (b) that I had never in fact been alive but had 'merely' been a robot. My concern has been to reveal this attitude as if not plainly absurd then at least unsupported by good arguments in its favour. My conclusion is that one day computers will meet all the criteria by which we recognize life forms and that when such a stage is reached it will be right to say that they are alive. The most sophisticated of the machines which we have today are the ancestors of these living machines and are entitled to be thought of (at least by future generations) as emergent life forms (rather like the primeval slime out of which we emerged), while machines like typeriters and motor cars are just that — machines.

6.4   INTRODUCTION

It is often (naively) thought that computers just do what their programs tell then to do and that they are not capable of making decisions in their own right. Thus a payroll computer doesn't 'decide' to pay Smith more than Jones but does so only because the instructions which it is following tell it to pay Smith more than Jones.

This picture of computer behaviour is deceptive. While it is true to say that computers follow the instructions which make up their programs and are not capable of doing anything which is not explicitly covered by the program, it is still not true to say that computers do not make decisions. Consider the following simple task suitable for a normal child of six: I will give you a number which I would like you to write down. When you have done this I will give you another number which you should also write down. Then I want you to tell me if the first number was larger than the second number. If all the numbers are kept smaller than ten then this should present little difficulty. There are three possible correct answers: the first is larger, the second is larger, the numbers are equal. The child must decide between these answers on the basis of the figures he has before him. Now here is a computer program to tackle the same problem.

```
10  INPUT first_number
20  INPUT second_number
30  IF first_number > second_number THEN PRINT "The first is larger"
    ELSE GOTO 50
40  END
50  IF first_number < second_number THEN PRINT "The second is larger"
    ELSE PRINT PRINT "The numbers are equal"
60  END
```

It seems fairly clear to me there is a strong case for saying that a computer following this program is making decisions. To be sure, the decisions are fairly low level but they are decisions none the less. One of the worries people feel about this example is that the computer does not appear to be free to go outside the dictates of the program to, for example, complain that the number game has become boring. My reply to this objection is that it does nothing more than point to the obvious fact that the choices open to a computer following the program in question are limited to three while those open to a child engaged in the same sort of task are more extensive, but the example was never intended to show the contrary. None of us ever has an infinite number of options to choose between — there are just so many options open to people at any given tine. Our reaction to this is not to say that we have no choice at all but to get on with making our decision. Similarly the computer has a choice, albeit a very limited one, and has a decision to make albeit a very trivial one.

6.4.1 Determinism

Another reaction to the above example cuts to the heart of our reluctance to accept that computers really do make choices. The position is as follows: the computer in the number game example is not making a real choice because when the numbers are given to it there is only one option left open. By contrast, the human child still has lots of options available after all the data is in: he can complain of boredom, of hunger, he can say that he would like to go and play with his friends now, and so on. The computer, a slave to the end, gets the data and prints out the only answer available to it. How different from the human case!

This response is, in essence, the familiar complaint that computer answers are, unlike human ones, completely predictable — that computers are subject to determinism but that human beings are free. Notice that the output of this simple program is not predictable in the abstract — we need to know all the data on which the program will be working before we are able to predict the response with accuracy. If two further lines are added:

25 random_number = RND(9)
26 IF first_number = random_number THEN PRINT "I'm tired of this game": END

then no one will be able to predict for sure what the computer will print out unless they know in advance what the computer's pseudo random number generator will give in response to line 25. So here we have a simple eight-line program with just three variables and already we are having to delve into the hardware of the machine running the program in order to predict the computer's responses. Bear in mind also that the program in question was not intended to show that computers can be free in the same way as you and I but only to demonstrate that computers can make very low-level decisions.

6.4.2 Computers with free will

I now propose to argue for the strong position that it is possible to program a machine so that it can make choices as freely as you and I do.

In the 1984 Reith lectures, John Searle characterizes the free-will problem as asking the question 'Is it ever true to say of a person that he could have done otherwise, all other conditions remaining the same?' If we answer 'yes' then we are affirming the existence of free will and otherwise denying it. Let's attempt this analysis on a fairly uncontroversial example of human action.

Yesterday I parked my car outside my office and left it unattended for no more than 90 seconds. When I returned, I discovered that someone had stolen one of my front spotlamps. We will call this miscreant Smith. Normally we should say that Smith freely chose to steal my lamp and that he is culpable for his behaviour. According to Searle, and, it should be said, almost everyone else, we can identify a moment at which Smith chose to steal my lamp and can debate the question of whether given the same set of circumstances Smith would again choose to steal from me. I think that Smith probably took my light because he had a similar set of his own but had damaged one of then in an accident. Not wanting to have to pay for a new one Smith then went on the prowl for a replacement. He went out armed with the necessary tools and when he saw my car his opportunity had come and he made off with my light.

Now let's run the proposed analysis. Just before Smith actually steals the lamp we will ask the question 'Is it true to say of him that he might not steal the lamp, all other considerations remaining the same? It seems to me that the answer is a decisive no. The free-will advocate would traditionally respond that I have denied that Smith freely chose to steal from me, which (I agree) sounds very implausible. How is it that I can maintain both that Smith freely chose to steal from me and that at the moment before his theft he could not have done anything else? Not being able to do anything else means there is no choice, doesn't it?

The way in which I propose to perform this philosophical balancing trick is really very simple. I reject that Smith chose to steal at the moment immediately prior to his stealing. I propose the following analysis of choice: choosing is not a single isolatable mental act which occurs immediately prior to a physical action but is an on-going process which cannot be completely distinguished from the circumstances which determine it.

Hence it is not appropriate to 'freeze' time just before Smith acts because, as should be obvious, Smith has already heavily committed himself to acting as he did. Consider the facts: Smith is a thief, Smith needs a spotlamp, Smith has prepared himself to steal such a light, Anderson parks his car right in front of Smith, Smith believes (correctly) that he can carry out the theft unobserved. Given all of this there is no reason to say that Smith would ever do other than he did. But notice that it is not just a question of going back further in time and freezing the action there. In the first place it would sound pretty peculiar to say that Smith chose to steal my lamp before I left home this morning, or at any time before he saw my car, and in the second place it would still remain open for us to carry out a similar analysis of (say) Smith's choosing to steal some lamp and so on.

What I am suggesting is that choosing is an activity extended in time and that, this being so, the traditional way of posing the free-will problem is misleading. Indeed, the way the problem is posed is the source of the free-will problem. With my analysis there is no problem with free will, for there is no moment at which it is true to say that Smith must choose to do what he did. Our feeling that we always have options open to us is explained by our not knowing in advance what the future has in store. Smith felt that he could steal a lamp from almost any car, but when mine appeared, and when no one seemed to be watching hin, and so on, the die was cast.

I distinguish free choice from other sorts of choice by saying that a choice is free when it is made in accordance with one's preferences. Thus if I offer Jones a choice between apple pie and cheesecake and Jones prefers cheesecake, Jones will, all other things being equal, choose cheesecake. His choice will be freely made but here again the choosing cannot be pinned down to a moment immediately prior to his taking. It has developed out of Jones's on-going assessment of the situation he is in — does anyone else want cheesecake? If so, are there enough pieces to go around? Is the cheesecake of good appearance? and so on. Given that none of these other considerations sway him Jones will always do what he has a preference for, and knowing what his taste is and that nothing else concerns Jones we can predict with certainty what Jones will do. Thus, there are situations in which we recognize a compelling factor (Jones's taste) and still acknowledge the choice as being free.

It is not necessary in order for a choice to be free that we have actually chosen what our preferences are, only that, given our preferences, we choose in accordance with them.

6.4.3 Conclusion

If my analysis of choice is correct then it seems pretty clear that no philosophical objection remains to saying that computers might be programmed to exercise free choice. Computers would be programmed with inbuilt preferences and behaviour patterns which could, to some extent, be modified as a result of the experience that the computer subsequently has. Of course the changes which the computer's program would undergo would already be explicitly set out in the original program but it would not be possible for anyone, in practice, to know what the program would look like after twenty years of operation.

The reason for this is that if the computer was to be capable of fully simulating human behaviour it would have to be sensitive to very small changes in its environment and would, like us, have to be capable of being affected by these environmental stimuli. Since no one could predict the exact nature of the environment in which the computer wold be placed, no one could know which parts of its program would come into operation. In brief, the computer's behaviour could only be precisely predicted given a complete description of its operation, a complete description of its situation (environment), a complete description of the effect each situation would have on the computer and a great deal of calculation. In other words we could predict the behaviour of such a computer in just those circumstances in which the determinists have always claimed human behaviour could be predicted.

I hope I have successfully, albeit very briefly, outlined why it is that the computer's admitted conformity to determinism should not be thought of as disqualifying it from being regarded as being genuinely free. On my analysis, there is no conflict between determinism and free will, and so there is no reason why a properly programmed computer or a normal human being should not exercise freedom in a deterministic world.

I should like to wind up this chapter and the book as a whole by indicating how the creation of intelligent free robots could lead to an extension of the scope of our moral concern. It should be obvious from my comments so far that I do not think that intelligent robots are on the verge of being developed, at least not robots which are as intelligent as human beings.

If and when such machines are developed their production could give rise to a number of interesting moral problems. Many of these problems concern the effect that robots would have on the quality of human life: how many people would be put out of work, how much responsibility dare we entrust to non-humans, and so on. But the most interesting moral developments would not directly concern humans at all.

There are two or possibly three main elements which combine to produce any computer or robot and which would also be present in future intelligent robots. In the first place there is hardware: the nuts and bolts out of which the robot is formed, which also includes all of the micro-chips inside the robot as well as the solder which holds them in place and so on. Next there is software: this is the set of ordered instructions which the hardware is designed to follow; in a compter this is stored as a pattern of electrical charges of varying magnitudes (currently a 'high' voltage is thought of as representing '1' and a 'low' voltage as representing '0', thus giving rise to the binary mathematics which underlies the operation of computers). Hardware is established at the factory where the computer is built. Software, by contrast, may be changed at will by the user of the computer (the programmer). Between these two elements there is a case to be made for inserting a third — firmware. Firmware can be thought of as either hardware which has in-built programming or software permanently stored.

Software is stored inside a computer in memory locations which, like a notebook written in pencil, can both be read and written over. The purists call this sort of memory RWM (read/write memory); it is more commonly known as RAM (readable and addressable memory). Firmware is stored in memory locations which can only be read and cannot be changed; this sort of memory is known as ROM (read-only memory). A typical piece of firmware is a MOS (machine operating system), which enables the computer to function, or a computer language such as BASIC, Pascal, FORTRAN, LISP or LOGO. Other pieces of firmware include special text-handling routines called word processors (this is written using a very simple one called Wordwise). The common denominator is that the software thus stored is required to be available as soon as the computer is switched on.

A robot would almost certainly need a vast amount of firmware, which would be fitted at the time of its construction. As I have already indicated, this programming would enable the computer to interact with its environment and to alter its software in response to changing circumstances, thus allowing the robot to develop a personality of its own. Presumably there would be some chips which were more important to the effective functioning of the robot than others, for example it is more important to have an MOS than a word processor.

Now suppose that robots were constructed in such a way that the most important parts were always assembled and positioned first. Further suppose that at the end of a successful assembly a robot was fully equipped to go into the world and function like a human being of ten years of age. Remember that we are talking about a machine which can legitimately be thought of as a representative of another species, a genuine life form in its own right which can think as well as you or I, which has interests, desires, fears and hopes and so on.

Now a question arises: is there any stage during the production process involved in building such a machine where it would be morally wrong to discontinue production and throw away the partly finished robot? It seems to me that the answer to this must be an emphatic 'yes', at least as long as we oppose even some human abortions. I suggest that such a discontinuation would represent a new sort of abortion and would have to be opposed. All the reasons which we give for opposing human abortion apply here in spades. There is no question of saving a life by letting the robot die. The robot could easily survive in the world as the equivalent of a human five-year-old and would already have all or most of the required ability to mature as the result of its experience. I will not further labour the point. Suffice it to say that this is one example of our moral consideration having to expand in order to take account of the existence of intelligent free robots.

Notes and references

CHAPTER 1 — WHAT COMPUTERS HAVE TO DO

[1] Turing, A. M., 'Computing machinery and intelligence', *Mind*, **LIX**, 236 (1950), pp. 433–460.
[2] Ibid., p. 436.
[3] Ibid., pp. 436–437.
[4] Ibid., p. 437.
[5] Ibid., p. 443.
[6] Ibid., p. 444.
[7] Ibid., p. 444.
[8] Ibid., p. 445.
[9] Ibid., pp. 445–446.
[10] Ibid., p. 446.
[11] Ibid., p. 446.
[12] Ibid., p. 447.
[13] Ibid., p. 447.
[14] Ibid., p. 447.
[15] Ibid., p. 450.
[16] Ibid., pp. 450–451.
[17] Ibid., p. 451.
[18] Ibid., p. 451.
[19] Ibid., pp. 451–452.
[20] Ibid., p. 452.
[21] Ibid., p. 452.
[22] Ibid., p. 453.
[23] Ibid., p. 454.
[24] Ibid., p. 454.
[25] Ibid., pp. 454–455
[26] Ibid., p. 455.
[27] Ibid., p. 456.
[28] Ibid., p. 460.

CHAPTER 2 — WHAT COMPUTERS SEEM TO DO

[1] Colby, K. M., 'Modeling a paranoid mind' *The Behavioral and Brain Sciences*, **4** (1981), p. 518.

[2] Ibid., p. 530.
[3] Ibid., pp. 528–529.
[4] Greenblatt, R. D., Eastlake, D. E., & Crocker, S. D., 'The Greenblatt chess program', *Proc. Fall Joint Computer Conference*, p. 802.
[5] Ibid., p. 802.
[6] Ibid., p. 802.
[7] Ibid., p. 803.
[8] Ibid., p. 803.
[9] Ibid., p. 801.

CHAPTER 3 — WHAT COMPUTERS CAN'T DO

[1] Dreyfus, H. L., 'Alchemy and artificial intelligence', The RAND Corporation, paper 3244 (December 1965).
[2] This ended up with 'Alchemy and artificial intelligence' being released in mimeograph form.
[3] Dreyfus, H. L., *What Computers Can't Do*, Harper & Row, New York (1979), p. 67.
[4] Hobbes, T., *Leviathan*, Library of Liberal Arts, New York (1958), p. 45.
[5] Dreyfus, H. L., *What Computers Can't Do*, p. 70.
[6] Ibid., p. 70.
[7] Ibid., p. 71.
[8] Ibid., pp. 73–74.
[9] See Newell, A., Shaw, J. C., & Simon, H. A., 'The processes of creative thinking', The RAND Corporation Paper 1320 (September 1958).
[10] Dreyfus, H. L., *What Computers Can't Do*, p. 83.
[11] Ibid., p. 83.
[12] Simon, H. A. and P. A., 'Trial and error in solving difficult problems: evidence from the game of chess', *Behavioral Sience*, **7** (1962), p. 429.
[13] See Greenblatt, R. D., Eastlake, D. E., & Crocker, S. D., 'The Greenblatt chess program', *Am. Fed. Inf. Proc. Soc. Proceedings Fall Joint Computer Conference* (1967), pp. 801–810.
[14] Dreyfus, H. L., *What Computers Can't Do*, p. 84.
[15] See Greenblatt, R. D., *et al.*, op. cit., p. 801 and pp. 808–809.
[16] Dreyfus, H. L., *What Computers Can't Do*, p. 99.
[17] Ibid., p. 156.
[18] Von Neumann, J., 'Probabilistic logics and the synbook of reliable organisms from unreliable components', in Taub, A. H. (ed.), *Collected Works*, New York (1963), Pergamon Press, Vol. 5, p. 372.
[19] Von Neumann, J., 'The general and logical theory of automata', in *The World of Mathematics*, New York (1956), Simon & Schuster, p. 2077.
[20] Dreyfus, H. L., *What Computers Can't Do*, p. 161.
[21] Ibid., p. 156.
[22] Ibid., p. 165.

[23] Ibid., p. 166.
[24] Ibid., p. 174, from Miller, Galanter and Pribram, *Plans and the Structure of Behavior*, New York (1960), Holt, Rinehart & Winston, p. 16.
[25] Ibid., p. 176.
[26] Ibid., p. 177.
[27] Ibid., pp. 177–178.
[28] Ibid., p. 178.
[29] Ibid., p. 180.
[30] Ibid., p. 187.
[31] Ibid., p. 156.
[32] Ibid., p. 195.
[33] Ibid., p. 198.
[34] Ibid., p. 198.
[35] Ibid., p. 199.
[36] Ibid., p. 199.
[37] However, I do not think that Dreyfus has it in mind to include unwarranted extensions of terms, for example:
'Smith: There are no good restaurants in Brighton.
Jones: Don't be silly, Brighton has lots of restaurants and many of them are good.
Smith: I don't count a restaurant as being good if there is a meal which the restaurant doesn't serve.
After all, it is precisely in such cases that humans cannot communicate effectively without further explanation.
[38] Dreyfus, H. L., *What Computers Can't Do*, p. 201.
[39] Ibid., p. 156.
[40] Minsky, M. L., *Semantic Information Processing*, Cambridge, Mass. (1968), MIT Press.
[41] Ibid., p. 26.
[42] Dreyfus, H. L., *What Computers Can't Do*, p. 217.
[43] Ibid., p. 214.
[44] Ibid., p. 222.
[45] Ibid., p. 222.
[46] Ibid., p. 236.
[47] Ibid., p. 237.
[48] Ibid., p. 239.
[49] Ibid., p. 241.
[50] Ibid., p. 242.
[51] Ibid., p. 242.
[52] Ibid., p. 249.
[53] Ibid., p. 252.
[54] Schank, R. C., 'Natural language, philosophy and artificial intelligence', in Ringle, M. D., (ed.), *Philosophical Perspectives in Artificial Intelligence*, p. 196.
[55] Ibid., p. 197.
[56] Ibid., p. 204.

[57] Ibid., pp. 204–205.
[58] Ibid., p. 205.
[59] Ibid., pp. 205–206.

CHAPTER 4 — WHAT SOME COMPUTERS CAN'T DO

[1] Searle, J. R., 'Minds, brains and programs', in *The Behavioral and Brain Sciences*, **3** (1980), reprinted in Dennett, D. C., and Hofstadter, D. R. (eds), *The Mind's I*, Brighton (1981), Harvester Press, pp. 353–373.

[2] Boden, M. A., *Artificial Intelligence and Natural Man*, Brighton (1977), Harvester Press, p. 5.

[3] Minsky, M. L., (ed.), *Semantic Information Processing*, Cambridge, Mass. (1968), MIT Press, p. V.

[4] Boden, M. A., op. cit., p. 5.

[5] Searle, J. R., op. cit., p. 353.

[6] Colby, K. M., 'Modelling a parenoid mind', *The Behavioral and Brain Sciences* (1981), pp. 515–560.

[7] Boden, M. A., op. cit., p. 97.

[8] Searle, J. R., 'The myth of the computer: an exchange', in *The New York Review of Books* (24th July 1982), p. 57.

[9] Searle, J. R., 'Minds brains and programs', p. 353.

[10] Marshall, J. C., 'Artificial intelligence — the real thing?', *The Behavioral and Brain Sciences*, **3** (1980), p. 436.

[11] Ibid., p. 436.

[12] Searle, J. R., 'Author's response', *The Behavioral and Brain Sciences*, **3** (1980), p. 455.

[13] Ibid., p. 455.

[14] Ibid., p. 455.

[15] Searle, J. R., 'Minds, brains and programs', p. 367.

[16] Actually Searle is playing for much bigger stakes — nothing less than a demonstration that the whole project of strong AI is doomed to failure.

[17] Searle, J. R., 'The myth of the computer', in *The New York Review of Books* (29th April 1982), p. 5.

[18] Searle, J. R., 'Minds, brains and programs', p. 356.

[19] Ibid., p. 355.

[20] Ibid., p. 355.

[21] Ibid., pp. 355–356.

[22] Ibid., p. 357.

[23] Ibid., p. 359.

[24] Ibid., p. 358.

[25] Ibid., p. 359.

[26] Ibid., p. 359.

[27] Dennett, D. C., 'The myth of the computer: an exchange', in *The New York Review of Books* (24th July 1982), p. 56.

[28] Searle, J. R., 'The myth of the computer: an exchange', in *The New York Review of Books* (24th July 1982), p. 56.

[29] Searle, J. R., 'Minds, brains and progams', pp. 358–359.
[30] The discussion which follows Searle's article in *The Mind's I* is actually only signed by Hofstadter, but I have chosen to attribute the views expressed to H&D jointly for the following reasons. Hofstadter constantly uses 'we' rather than 'I' when putting forward his case, and when Searle objected to the misquotation in the commentary it was Dennett who replied. In Dennett's discussion 'we' is also used in preference to 'I' and throughout he is clearly speaking of Hofstadter as well.
[31] Hofstadter, D. R., and Dennett, R. C., *The mind's I*, Brighton (1981), Harvester Press, p. 375.
[32] Ibid., p. 377.
[33] Ibid., p. 378.
[34] See McCarthy, J., 'Ascribing mental qualities to machines', in Ringle, M. D., (ed.), *Philosophical Perspectives in Artificial Intelligence*, Brighton (1979), Harvester Press.
[35] Searle, J. R., 'Minds, brains and programs', pp. 361–362.
[36] By the same token, a cloud shedding rain is presumably showing that it has a belief that the ground below is too dry!
[37] Searle, J. R., 'Minds, brains and programs', p. 362.
[38] Ibid., p. 358.
[39] Ibid., p. 362.
[40] Ibid., p. 362.
[41] Ibid., p. 363.
[42] Ibid., pp. 363–364.
[43] Ibid., p. 364.
[44] Ibid., p. 364.
[45] Ibid., p. 365.
[46] Ibid., p. 366.
[47] Ibid., p. 366.
[48] Ibid., p. 366.
[49] Ibid., p. 369.
[50] Searle, J. R., 'The myth of the computer', p. 4.
[51] Searle, J. R., 'Minds, brains and programs', p. 367.
[52] Ibid., p. 367.
[53] Ibid., p. 367.
[54] Ibid., p. 357.
[55] Ibid., p. 368.
[56] Ibid., p. 370.
[57] Walter, D. O., 'The thermostat and the philosophy professor', in *The Behavioral and Brain Sciences*, 3, (1980), p. 449.
[58] Searle, J. R., The Myth of the computer, p. 4.
[59] Pylyshyn, Z. W., 'The "causal power" of machines', in *The Behavioral and Brain Sciences*, 3 (1980), p. 442.
[60] Searle, J. R., *'Minds, brains and programs'*, (1980), p. 371.

[61] Ibid., p. 371.
[62] Ibid., pp. 371–372.

CHAPTER 5 — A CLASSICAL PROBLEM

[1] Quine, W. V. O., 'On what there is', reprinted in *From a Logical Point of View*, Cambridge, Mass. (1980), Harvard, p. 18.
[2] Kleene, S. C., *Metamathematics*, Amsterdam (1952).
[3] Lukasiewicz, J., 'On three valued logic' (1920), in McCall, S. (ed.), *Polish Logic*, Oxford (1967).
[4] Asenjo, F. G., 'A calculus of antinomies', *Notre Dame Journal of Formal Logic* (1966), 497–509.
[5] Priest, G., 'The logic of paradox', *Journal of Philosophical Logic* (1979), p. 226.
[6] Ibid., p. 226.
[7] Ibid., p. 227.
[8] Ibid., pp. 227–228.
[9] Ibid., p. 228.
[10] Ibid., p. 235.
[11] Ibid., p. 235.
[12] Ibid., p. 236.
[13] Flew, A., *A Dictionary of Philosophy* (1979), p. 203.
[14] Priest, G., op. cit., p. 237.
[15] Lewis, D., 'Logic for equivocators', read at La Trobe, June 1980, and ANU, July 1980, p. 1.
[16] Ibid., p. 3.
[17] Ibid., p. 4.
[18] Ibid., p. 4.
[19] Ibid., p. 5.
[20] Ibid., p. 6.
[21] Ibid., pp. 6–7.
[22] Ibid., p. 7.
[23] Ibid., p. 8.
[24] Ibid., pp. 9–10.
[25] Ibid., p. 13.

CHAPTER 6 — LIVING WITH COMPUTERS

[1] Wiener, N., *The Human Use of Human Beings*, New York (1954), p. 46.
[2] Berrill, N. J., *Biology in Action*, London, (1967).
[3] Ovenden, M., in Young, L. B., *The Mystery of Matter*, New York (1965), pp. 540–541.
[4] Lorenz, K., *Evolution and the Modification of Behaviour*, Chicago (1965), p. 32.

[5] Wiener, N., op. cit., p 95.
[6] Sayer, K. M., *Cybernetics and the Philosophy of Mind*, London (1976), p. 89.
[7] Ibid., p. 89.
[8] Simons, G., *Are computers alive?*, Brighton (1983), p. 12.
[9] Sayer, K. M., op. cit., p. 91.
[10] Ibid., p. 50.
[11] Ibid., p. 50.
[12] Ibid., p. 50.
[13] Ibid., pp. 50–51.

Select bibliography

Asenjo, F. G. (1966), 'A calculus of antinomies', *Notre Dame Journal of Formal Logic*, pp. 497–509.

Berrill, N. J. (1967), *Biology in Action*, London.

Boden, M. A. (1977), *Artificial Intelligence and Natural Man*, Brighton, Harvester Press.

Colby, K. M. (1981), 'Modelling a paranoid mind', *The Behavioral and Brain Sciences*, **4**.

Dennett, D. C. (1982) 'The myth of the computer: an exchange', *The New York Review of Books*, 24th July.

Dennett, D. C., and Hofstadter, D. R. (eds) (1981), *The Mind's I*, Brighton, Harvester Press.

Dreyfus, H. L. (1965). 'Alchemy and artificial intelligence', The RAND Corporation, Paper 3244 (December).

Dreyfus, H. L. (1979) *What computers Can't Do*, Harper & Row, New York.

Flew, A. (1979), *A Dictionary of Philosophy*,

Greenblatt, R. D., Eastlake, D. E., and Crocker, S. D. (1967), 'The Greenblatt chess program', *Am. Fed. Inf. Proc. Soc. Proceedings Fall Joint Computer Conference*, pp. 801–810.

Hobbes, T. (1958), *Leviathan*, Library of Liberal Arts, New York.

Kleene, S. C. (1952), *Metamathematics*, Amsterdam.

Lewis, D. (1980), 'Logic for equivocators, read at La Trobe, June, and ANU, July.

Lorenz, K. (1965), *Evolution and the Modification of Behavior*, Chicago.

Lukasiewicz, J. (1920), On three valued logic' in McCall, S. (ed.), *Polish Logic*, Oxford (1967).

Marshall, J. C. (1980), 'Artificial intelligence–the real thing?', *The Behavioral and Brain Sciences*, **3**.

McCarthy, J. (1979), 'Ascribing mental qualities to machines', in Ringle, M. D., (ed.) *Philosophical Perspectives in Artifical Intelligence*, Brighton.

Miller, Galanter and Pribram (1960), *Plans and the Structure of Behavior*, New York, Holt, Rinehart & Winston.

Minsky, M. L. (ed.) (1968), *Semantic Information Processing*, Cambridge, Mass., MIT Press.

Newell, A., Shaw, J. C., and Simon, H. A. (1958) 'The processes of creative thinking', The RAND Corporation, Paper 1320 (September).

Ovenden, M., (1965), in Young, L. B. (ed.), *The Mystery of Matter*, New York.

Priest, G. (1979), 'The logic of paradox, *Journal of Philosophical Logic*, **8**.

Pylyshyn, Z. W. (1980), 'The "causal power" of machines', *The Behavioural and Brain Sciences, 3*.

Quine, W. V. O. (1980), 'On what there is', reprinted in *From a Logical Point of View*, Cambridge, Mass., Harvard.

Sayre, K. M. (1976), *Cybernetics and the Philosophy of Mind*, London.

Schank, R. C., 'Natural language, philosophy and artificial intelligence', in Ringle, M. D., (ed.), *Philosophical Perspectives in Artificial Intelligence*,

Searle, J. R. (1980), 'Author's response', *The Behavioral and Brain Sciences*, **3**.

Searle, J. R. (1980), 'Minds, brains and programs', *The Behavioral and Brain Sciences*, **3**.

Searle, J. R. (1982) 'The myth of the computer', in *The New York Review of Books*, (29th April).

Searle, J. R. (1982), 'The myth of the computer: an exchange', in *The New York Review of Books*, (24th July).

Simon, H. A. and Simon, P. A. (1962), 'Trial and error in solving difficult problems: evidence from the game of chess', *Behavioral Science*, **7** (October).

Simons, G., (1983), *Are Computers Alive*, Brighton.

Turing, A. M. (1950), 'Computing machinery and intelligence, *Mind*, **LIX**.

Index